A Locust Leaves
Its Shell

A Locust Leaves
Its Shell

*Collected columns
by Bill Easterling*

Edited by Mike Kaylor

Published in the United States of America

*This book is for Pat, my wife,
my best friend. She never lets
me down, and although I think
she's too beautiful to be hidden,
she always stands back and lets
me shine. I'd have wasted my life
if she hadn't helped me
change my ways.*

Acknowledgments

This book has been made possible because Publisher Bob Ludwig and Editor Joe Distelheim gave it their blessings and allowed me to use copyrighted material from *The Huntsville Times*.

I also want to thank *Times* graphic artist Dulcie Teesateskie for designing the book's attractive cover. Jenny Kaylor saved the day when she sat down at her home computer and typed in several columns which couldn't be found in *The Times'* electronic library. Thanks to John Shaver for giving the book a last look before publication. And, of course, my dear friend, mentor, editor and publisher, Mike Kaylor, has again done the hard, thankless technical work of putting a book together for me.

This project wouldn't have been possible without those people, and I thank them very much.

Introduction

When I introduced "Voices On a Cold Day" in 1986, I wanted it to be the first in a trilogy of books featuring a collection of the human interest columns I write for *The Huntsville Times.*

Well, 14 years after the first book appeared, the second installment, "A Locust Leaves Its Shell," has finally gone to press.

I might have continued to procrastinate, or maybe have decided not to put another book of columns together period, if concerns about my own mortality hadn't suddenly popped up in the summer of 1999.

So, with the gentle encouragement of family, friends and a new crop of readers I've cultivated since "Voices" first appeared, I dove headlong into a decade of newspaper columns, trying to pick out some I thought would fit what my idea of my column is all about.

This is certainly not intended to be a "best of" collection of columns. But it is a mixture of what I believe describes what my editors and publishers have always expected of me. Although you'll recognize some names as famous, these columns are mostly about the so-called "common"' people, those who make up the majority of humanity and who mostly never get their names in the paper unless it's in an obituary.

In the introduction to my first book of collected columns, I said I couldn't take this personal stroll through dreamland if people like you weren't interested enough to read what I write.

I also said I've always been flattered, honored and humbled to be invited into your lives, and that I'd quit if I ever started taking those visits lightly.

Nothing has changed on either count.

The columns in this book appear as they were originally written, so many of the people and places described may now be only memories.

If it's God's will, the trilogy will be completed and there will one day be a third, and final, collection of these columns, the writing of which has sustained and strengthened me on days when I have not wanted to get out of bed.

If it is God's will, I promise this time there won't be 14 years between editions.

Bill Easterling
September, 2000

Table of Contents

I. Getting Personal

Angels We Have Heard on High

The best present I got for Christmas was being with my family. Pants sag and shirts shrink, but there's no need to keep a refund slip for the gift of family. It's a perfect fit every time.

This is for those who've lost loved ones. It's for those with husbands, wives, sons or daughters in the armed forces who're in harm's way. It's for those who made sure the children of the poor had toys, too.

The newest member of my family is too small to understand what the season's all about. She does, however, love the lights wrapped around the trees. She's fascinated by their brightness, and a sure way to calm her down when she's a little too rowdy is to have her watch them blinking.

"Light," she softly says, mostly to herself.

So, too, does the oldest member of my family love the lights of Christmas, and though she's long since quit being fascinated by them, their presence also has a calming effect on her.

That's because the lights remind her of the star that rose above a certain manger in biblical Bethlehem. Therefore, the bright lights of Christmas help her face the incontrovertible fact of old age. I know this to be true because she has told me many times.

My mother is an old, old woman and my granddaughter is a very young child, and somewhere in between is where my essence is and what my existence is about.

In addition to my mother and granddaughter, I have two brothers, a son, a stepson, a daughter, a stepdaughter, a son-in-law, a daughter-in-law and several nieces and nephews of whom I am awfully fond.

There was a time when I thought my reason for being was to write about people who otherwise wouldn't get their names in the newspaper unless it was in an obituary.

My perspective was suddenly altered when my mother abruptly grew quite old at about the same time my granddaughter was born. Since these events took place almost simultaneously, I decided my priorities might need rearranging. I began to view my family in a different way.

What if death swiftly took one of them away from me? What if one of them was sent across the world to do a job and could not communicate with me every day? What would I do and how would I feel if something happened to me and I couldn't afford to buy them presents at Christmas?

Those sorrowful, dreadful things happen to people every day, but the rest of us seldom pay attention until it's our turn.

My turn will likely come sooner than later, and I was never more aware of that than when I watched the crooked, loving fingers of the oldest member of my family reach out to touch the soft, smooth face of her great-granddaughter while the lights of a Christmas tree blinked behind them.

(December 26, 1996)

I Suppose He'd Still Be Waiting

The first thing I did when I became sports editor of *The Huntsville Times* was call my parents. It was a Saturday, and I wanted to tell them the story would be in Sunday's paper. My mother Eleanor was happiest, I suppose because she felt my excitement on the phone.

She congratulated me and told me how proud she was, though I'm sure at the time she didn't know a thing about any sports editor. When she handed my father the phone and I repeated what had happened, he responded with one of the greatest one-liners I've ever been privileged to hear.

He said: "Maybe you can do that until you get a real job."

I almost forgot, but a couple of weeks ago was the 25th anniversary of his death. He died March 4, 1967, at the age of 63. That's not old by today's standards. But in those days it seemed like he was an old man to me.

I guess that's because of the life he had to live. His folks were dirt poor and he never got far away from it. Uneducated people usually don't. But he made up for what he lacked in formal education with common sense, his finishing school being the Great Depression and a piece of bottom land he sharecropped.

The only photograph I have of him is the way I remember him most: high cheekbones, flashing dark eyes behind wire-rimmed glasses, black hair graying at the temples and combed straight back with a part in the middle. He's smiling a forced smile in the photograph, which accentuates the wrinkles in his Indian-heritage face.

He named me after himself, but nobody called him Bill. His brothers and sisters called him by his middle name, Rhodes. Everybody else just called him Slim, which is what they usually call a man who's 6-2, 135.

The other day on one of those rare occasions when I visited his grave I thought about the paradox of 25 years. A quarter of a century can be both a long time and a short time, for although many things have happened to me since that day in 1967 it seems like it wasn't long ago at all when six of his friends carried him to his final resting place. The medical report said a broken blood vessel in his head killed him, but I think life was what did it.

I'm sorry, too, because he and I had just begun to understand each other, and his four grandchildren had just begun to grow.

Now the grandchildren are grown, there are

three great-grandchildren, and all any of them have are a few fuzzy memories and a picture on a wall in my mother's house.

Unless, of course, they get their grandmother to tell some stories about him, which, if they do, I hope they ask about the bad as well as the good.

I say that because I know he wouldn't have it any other way, wouldn't want to be painted pearly white when in actuality there was lots of gray, and he would, if he could, kick my butt from sunup to sundown for writing about him in the paper.

Twenty-five years. So long ago. Yet not so far away.

He went to the third grade, but once told me Russia wouldn't survive because "they sharecroppers don't get enough." He would have known.

If he was here, I guess he'd still try to tell my brothers Ed and Charles the best way to do things. And knowing him, I guess he'd still be waiting for me to get a real job.

(March 24, 1992)

Memories of a Boy I Knew
on Some Hot Summer Days

He was buried on the kind of summer day we woke up hoping for as kids. I closed my eyes and thought of that while the sound of "Ave Maria" filled the chapel at his funeral.

Carried along by the stirring rhapsody of such an inspiring piece of music, my mind drifted to those golden August days of boyhood when school was just ahead and a season of loafing was right behind.

The only decision we had to make on those hot, sunny days with blue skies above us and green grass below us was what we were going to do with our time. We played baseball almost every afternoon. Shove-up was a favorite game when we didn't have enough for teams. But three to a side was usually enough to play Yankees versus Dodgers in our version of the World Series.

Tired and sweaty from the baseball, we often crossed the highway and made our way through a pasture to a stock pond where we stripped naked and swam in muddy water. Some days we hiked through cotton fields to the Tennessee River a couple of miles away, stirring up dust with our bare feet, enjoying how the hot dirt felt between our toes.

There were seven of us who usually stuck together: Buddy, Harvey, Jackie, Tommy, Wayne, Frankie and me. Frankie was the youngest, and maybe the most determined, and he was the one we protected most. As the swirling melody of "Ave Maria" came to a close, I saw him crouched at the plate, jaw set, bat cocked, his eyes peering out from under the bill of his cap.

Frank James Beasley grew up to be a police detective. Maybe it was because we were so good at sneaking around and doing things we shouldn't have done when we were kids. Maybe it was because of that sage field he and I didn't mean to set afire.

Whatever the reason, he spent most of his adult life being one of the good guys, and if he'd lived a little longer, he'd have served 25 years on the force.

It doesn't matter to those who knew him that his name won't be on any street signs or monuments, since he didn't die in the line of duty. It does matter that the men and women of law enforcement he served with respected his work as a detective and his beliefs as a man and will keep his memory alive in their hearts.

I wish I could say something today to make the suffering go away from his family and friends. But

10

I can't. Only time heals, and only those who suffer such losses ever know how much time it takes to mend a broken heart.

What I do know is Frankie and his family played big roles in the formative years of my life. His parents have been like a father and a mother to me. They encouraged me to reach beyond my grasp, and I did, knowing they'd be among those there to catch me if I fell. Something else crossed my mind as the soaring music filled the funeral hall: Frankie was proud to wear the shield of a detective.

The shrinking little band of boys he shared those summers with is proud of him, too.

(August 24, 1997)

Goodbye to a Man Who Wasn't Just a Friend

We carried him in a flag-draped coffin to his dusty grave on a September afternoon so hot the funeral director handed out umbrellas for shade. It was the kind of day he would have loved all those years ago when he and I played 18 holes of golf in no more than three hours at the almost-flat, mostly treeless old municipal course.

We played "ready" golf: first one to his ball went ahead and hit. Because we walked (I carried my bag on my back, he pulled his on a cart), ready golf was how we were able to play such fast rounds on my so-called "lunch hour."

I was the paper's sports editor then and he was a retired firefighter who had worked with my father at Redstone Arsenal.My dad died in 1967 when I was 26, but my golfing partner helped fill the empty place I felt in my heart for the next several years.

He had three sons of his own, but he always had time for me. I had so many thoughts about him at his funeral Thursday, they were buzzing around in my head like bees.

Should I tell about showing up at his house

with one of my mother's fried apple pies in my hip pocket and sitting on his nice, clean couch when I was a kid? Should I confess about how his oldest boy and I accidentally set a field afire near our homes and our fathers rode the truck that answered the call?

He forgave me for my childhood thoughtlessness. But why not? Those blunders provided him plenty of ammunition years later whenever he wanted to put me in my place in front of my adult friends. He liked going with me to watch Alabama and Auburn play football. I liked having him along. I asked many questions about stuff I wasn't sure of when we were driving back from those games, and his answers were always encouraging.

He wasn't the kind of man who wears his feelings on his sleeve, so I had forgotten about his military service until seeing the red, white and blue American flag covering his coffin.

Because he had always been such a hero to me, I felt it was fitting for this plain and simple no-nonsense man whose head was filled with common sense to be given such an honor by the country he served.

Frank O. Beasley was many things. Extravagant wasn't one of them. During all of those times we played together, he seldom used a new golf ball unless he found one that had been lost.

He could get more rounds out of a ball than anybody who ever played the game. And if he happened to be using one of his better balls when he reached a water hole, he always put an older one down. Lots of us who played with him later wished we'd done the same.

So when the coffin was opened to let his wife, Carrie, his surviving sons, Robert and Ronnie, and the rest of the family say goodbye, I slipped him a sleeve of brand new Titleist golf balls to use when he reaches the first tee in heaven.I just wanted to give him something special to take there with him because he left so much here for me.

(September 20, 1998)

They Didn't Respond
to Shakespeare

Naturally, somebody wanted to know if physical education was my favorite subject in high school after a recent column explained how I felt about algebra. Not even close. Even the cafeteria lunch rated much higher with me, and for one good reason. Coach Clem Gryska taught P.E.

He was the football coach and good enough to be hired by Paul "Bear" Bryant at Alabama. He was also to the right of Attila the Hun. I hope none of my classmates sends this to Coach Gryska.

Here was a man who took the job seriously. He actually thought he was supposed to make winners out of weenies in P.E. class. We had to take tests every six weeks. We lifted weights. We climbed ropes to the rafters of the gym. We did pushups, chinups, and, on several occasions, throwups.

And we boxed. He made the matches. That's because he knew we always got together and tried to pair up and fix the fights. You know ... we'll make it look good, but we won't draw blood. Didn't work. Heavyweights fought flyweights, and etc. And if you bled, you got a better mark in Coach

Gryska's grade book whether you won or lost. Now that I think about it, Coach knew what a P.E. class is really supposed to be.

We all cried when he went to Alabama. They were tears of happiness. Later, when I wrote sports and saw him at Crimson Tide practices, he'd smile his crooked grin and ask if I'd had any good fights lately.

My favorite courses were biology and chemistry. Like algebra, I've never used anything I learned in those classes since I last took them in 1958. Unlike algebra, they were some of the most fun I've ever had.

Why is easy to explain.

Where else can a teen-aged boy attempt to blow up the school legally if not in chemistry class? We must have cost the school system a bundle in glass beakers. We must have caused several teachers and an office full of administrators to almost have heart attacks. We must have caused the school board to pay dearly for insurance.

But it was real thrilling when somebody yelled "Hit the deck!" and we dove under the tables just before one of our frequent explosions. Teachers ran from the rooms to help pull bodies from the rubble, the fire alarm sounded, somebody got threatened with expulsion.

Hey, and we had several guys who went on to become engineers, but because I like them so much, I won't tell you which bridges and buildings they helped construct.

And where else can a teen-aged boy have some of the prettiest girls in school drape themselves around his neck if not in biology class? I loved that dissecting business. Frogs, worms, whatever. I always wondered what would happen if just one day they'd have let us dissect a cadaver.

Girls who normally wouldn't look at you in the halls would grab you by the arm and hold on tight for 60 minutes as soon as we started to cut those things apart. I was a skinny, knock-kneed, crew-cut jangle of nerves, myself, and kind of liked being fell upon by blondes, brunettes, and redheads when the knives were being wielded.

That never happened when I recited Shakespeare.

And certainly didn't when I explained why pi r square in algebra class.

(November 1, 1990)

That Thing Is History and More

"What's that thing?" asked a young reporter. The "thing" is in a corner of a main hallway at The Times where traffic's heaviest, making it an item of interest among those who've never seen one before. In fact, only employees who've been around for a couple of decades know what it is. Younger ones don't have a clue, since the only journalism they know comes out of a computer.

What the reporter asked about is an unfinished reconstruction of a linotype machine, which, when finished, will be part of a newspaper museum we've talked about having for years. Linotype made it possible for newspapers to go to press when computers were only somebody's dream. Monday when I saw the skeleton of one being put together, memories of 33 years of being a paperman fought for equal space in my mind. I was happy when I heard one had been bought from a local printer so it could be spruced up and used as a museum piece, because all of ours have been long gone and I figured we'd never see one again.

When it's finished and finally displayed, the

"hot metal" era of newspapering will come alive again. And young reporters will really be able to get a good laugh then. This is an abbreviated version of how The Times was put together back then:

Reporters wrote stories on manual typewriters (Underwood and Royal being the preferred brands), editors made changes with red pencils, and copy carriers (I was the very first one) took those stories to the composing room where the big, black Mergenthaler Co. linotype machines sat all in a row.

They had typewriter-like keyboards. A chain hung from a steel arm. Attached to the chain was an ingot of lead, which hung over a bubbling, boiling pot. The pot was kept at 535-degrees Fahrenheit so it could melt the lead. The melted, molten lead, you see, was the "paper" linotype operators typed words on -- thus the term hot metal.

Nobody ever got scalded or badly burned, but there were always some blisters. Needless to say, schools weren't encouraged to visit very often, and when they did children were kept well away from those cauldrons.

I can still see faces of people who operated our linotype machines, and those who still work at The Times have had fun explaining about "that thing" in our hall. After stories typed with the hot metal process cooled, makeup men (there were no women doing that job) then put them in their proper columns in "magazines," which were the size of newspaper pages. After that, imprints were made on a cardboard-like substance, which was itself run through another furnace and turned into a metal cast which was bent to fit rollers of the press.

It was an astonishingly slow process, surely antiquated, and enough to make modern journalists scratch their heads in disbelief. But once upon a time it was the way every newspaper in the world went to press. That old thing being assembled in the hallway is both heritage and history of print journalism, and I'm pleased one was found to be saved.

Seeing it makes me smell printer's ink, feel it under my nails, taste it in the back of my throat. That was back when people were in control.

(June 17, 1992)

Some Wisdom in the Still
of the Night

I couldn't decide whether it was the pitiful way arbitration treated Bo Jackson or if the spaghetti sauce had been too thick, but I couldn't sleep. Toss, turn. Fluff pillows. Kick cover. Pretty soon me and everything else on the bed were in a wad.

So I gave up, got up and looked up an old friend. He was where I left him the last time we had a late-night chat. Top shelf, center, bookcase on the right.

Hello, sir, I said. I hope I am not disturbing you. "Thou art to me a delicious torment," said Ralph Waldo Emerson.

I said, "I wouldn't have bothered you, sir, but I couldn't sleep no matter how hard I tried."

He said, "Do what we can, summer will have its flies. If we walk in the woods, we must feed mosquitoes."

I said, "Sir, I think the arbitrator thought Bo asked for too much baseball money because he also gets football and endorsement money."

Emerson said, "A foolish consistency is the hobgoblin of little minds, adored by little statesmen and philosophers and divines."

I said, "Do you think, sir, Bo would do better if he just stuck to one sport?"

He said, "Whoso would be a man must be a non-conformist."

I said, "Well, that's certainly him, but I still don't think the arbitrator understood what Bo's all about."

"To be great is to be misunderstood," Ralph Waldo observed.

I said, "Then you think, sir, Bo will be vindicated in the end?"

He said, "Every hero becomes a bore at last."

Fearing this subject was wearing thin and becoming acutely aware the spaghetti sauce probably was the true source of my sleeplessness, I changed course.

I said, "Should I bring our friend Whitman into the discussion, sir?" (Knowing how he had patiently guided Walt through his early years.)

"Two may talk and one may hear, but three cannot take part in a conversation of the most sincere and searching sort," R.W.E. responded.

So I left Walt on the shelf and carried on.

"What do you think about all this unseasonable weather, sir?" I asked.

"Nature is a mutable cloud which is always and never the same," he answered.

Then I burped, apologized, told him I thought it was something I ate and allowed as how I should have taken something for the acid.

"Nothing can bring you peace but yourself," he noted.

To show him I kept up with the news of the day, I asked what he thought about recent events in East Europe and South Africa.

"The less government we have, the better -- the fewer laws and the less confided power," Emerson said.

I said there has been a literal showering, a veritable outpouring of emotion and heroism by the peoples of those places.

Ralph W. said, "Nothing great was ever achieved without enthusiasm."

It had gotten late. I asked if he had something, some favorite passage to help put me to sleep.

He said: "By the rude bridge that arched the flood

"Their flag to April's breeze unfurled.

"Here once the embattled farmers stood.

"And fired the shot heard round the world."

"Good, sir," I said, and yawned and turned to go.

At the foot of the stairs he called my name. Peering through the dim light, I saw a smile break across his gaunt, scraggy face. And Emerson told me to remember this:

"Every man is wanted, and no man is wanted much."

(February 6, 1990)

Willie Goes Back to First Grade

Almost 50 years after the other time, I went back to first grade Wednesday. One of my classmates wore shoes whose heels would light up when he walked.

"Hernandez," I said, "what do you call those shoes?" and he said, "Light-up shoes." Now I don't have to go around wasting lots of breath calling them "battery-operated shoes."

Because Montview Elementary School Principal Dr. Evelyn Pratt allowed me to attend Mrs. Ann Wright's first-grade class, I learned plenty on the first day of school this time that maybe I didn't learn that other time. Well, it was a long time ago.

This is some of what I learned:

-- Don't smudge the computer screen with my fingers.

--Talk in a very soft voice.

--Always sit up straight and nice and keep my feet on the floor.

--Raise my hand and get permission before talking.

I can say "yes" or "yes ma'am" but not "yeah."

--Keep my hands by my side while I walk.

--Keep my hands to myself.

I learned a poem about trains: "engine, engine No. 9, riding down the Huntsville line."

And a song about wheels: "The wheels on the bus go round and round, round and round, round and round, the wheels on the bus go round and round, all through town." I don't remember what I learned the first time I went to first grade, but I don't think I learned that poem and that song.

I know I didn't learn to hug classmates who weren't white because only white children went to school with me the first time I was in first grade. But though we were all different colors we still hugged each other and said bye after our first day of school Wednesday.

First grade was more fun this time for the simple reason I do remember the school I went to half a century ago didn't have a cafeteria and we ate what our mothers put in our brown paper lunch bags. This time, instead of bringing something from home I ate lunchroom food. And I sure didn't head for that salad bar some of the teachers headed for. I had a barbecue sandwich, Tater Tots and orange sherbet, thank you very much, and don't anybody tell my mother.

I learned schools are drowning in paperwork caused by government red tape, that schools with fewer students per teacher are very lucky and that good teachers still impact children in a positive way.

This time when I went to the principal's office,

it was much nicer than I remember the last time being. I learned about "Lefty" the octopus, whose big rule is "raise your hand" to get permission to talk.

I had my own name tag, shaped like a train, and my own desk. But I had to give the desk to an extra student who showed up for class. Something else I learned: Crowded classrooms aren't too much fun.

Before school Wednesday morning, while with some new friends I made, I also saw for the first time in my life a locust leave its shell, grow a pair of wings right before my eyes and climb off up a pine tree.

I met some good boys and girls I won't forget, even if Hernandez wouldn't let me wear those pretty light-up shoes of his, and I liked the teachers a lot, even if Mrs. Wright made me throw my chewing gum away before I came to class.

I learned many things on my first day of school that this time I won't forget. Not bad for the oldest first grader in town, huh?

(August 18, 1994)

We'd All Have Chicken in the Pot

If I could be in charge of 1992:

Rain would only fall between midnight and 4 a.m., and the sun would always shine on days ending with "y."

People with plenty to eat wouldn't quit trying until people who're starving got fed.

Anybody who wanted to quit smoking could without having to put up with any suffering.

High things, like cholesterol, blood pressure and the price of pills, would be outlawed.

Old people wouldn't be forgotten, young people wouldn't be ignored, and everybody would be treated with respect.

Good teachers would be encouraged to stay in education.

Everybody would learn how to read.

I'd be able to eat blackened redfish again.

Shrimp wouldn't be chock-full of cholesterol.

Skin cancer would take a vacation.

Everybody would have to look at themselves in the mirror first before making fun of people who wear pot-bellied shirts.

But, then, we'd all have flat stomachs. Diets would be banned. The correct terminology would be "I'm watching what I eat." Watching-what-I-eat jokes would be banned.

The Atlanta Braves would be National League pennant contenders again, 'cause they made last summer so much fun.

Nobody would get drunk then drive a vehicle because all drunks would miraculously decide they want to be sober, which would save lots of lives and many families.

Parents would replace rock stars and athletes as role models for children.

Ford and Chevrolet would start making the best cars and trucks in the world again.

My golf buddies would always give me the best bet on the first tee.

If I could be in charge of 1992:

No matter what their color, people would be judged by their character.

It'd be OK for me to eat a big portion of chocolate cake and vanilla ice cream now and then.

Crime would call a moratorium.

Either dogs would run free like cats or cats would be penned up like dogs.

People wouldn't throw trash on the streets, and people who saw any would stop and pick it up.

There'd be a ceiling on how much a pair of child's shoes could cost, and you wouldn't have to be tall to touch the ceiling.

Educating the young would be our most important priority.

Older men could again eat bowls of chili and not get heartburn.

An amazing new dinosaur graveyard would be discovered, possibly in New Mexico, and gasoline prices would fall so fast we'd all think it was 1970 again.

Fat-free French fries would be invented, then a grant would be given for a study to be made concerning low-cal prime rib.

Everybody everywhere would be happy for 12 months. For the next 365 days, I'd even like people I don't like, but not all of them. No student's report card would have an F on it, and there wouldn't be an awful lot of Ds, either.

People wouldn't have insomnia, but if they didn't want to sleep, they'd still feel good in the morning. Homemade ice cream wouldn't be bad for you in the months of June, July and August.

Everybody would be good money managers, and we'd all be out of debt by 1993, at which time I'd have to decide if I wanted to be in charge again. And I'd decide to do that except for one thing: If I could be in charge of 1992, I'd win the Florida lottery one of those weeks when it's worth $30 million.

(January 1, 1992)

On a Day When
Awesome Was Explained

KENNEDY SPACE CENTER, Fla. -- Now I know how Adam felt the first time he saw Eve, and what Moses thought when he got the tablets, and why adjectives were invented.

On a cloudy, windy Monday afternoon, with the setting sun a red dot through the Atlantic Ocean haze, we rode a bus three miles down a road past sand dunes and scrub brush to a hump on Cape Canaveral's back made of concrete and steel and called Launch Pad 39-B. And there, across a brackish marsh half a mile away, in all of its glory, stood STS-31.

Chained to its service structure, Space Shuttle Discovery waited for Tuesday morn to dawn so it could be shot into space on a scheduled journey to orbit history's most awaited telescope. (With today's scrub, though, that will have to wait awhile.)

For a first-time, hands-on observer, NASA's sundown press tour revealed what television can't, the magnitude of America's space program.

Seen through the naked eye from 900 yards away, the launch site reeked of raw power awaiting release.

There towered the rust-colored external fuel tank with the two white boosters and whiter shuttle strapped to its sides.

And there, in twilight's last gleaming, with sea birds losing a battle against 20-knot winds, workers on catwalks taking care of last-hours things were like ants on a sidewalk.

But through a 600-millimeter Minolta camera lens manned by a NASA photographer, if there'd been an astronaut in Discovery's cabin, you could have seen his face in the window.

Later, after dark and with the pad bathed in light, they took us 400 yards closer, and it was then the power and the glory of the event sank in.

Discovery's mission is to orbit the dream of a man named Edwin Powell Hubble -- a spyglass powerful enough to penetrate far out into the dark cavern of space when it's orbited 380 miles above Earth.

The Hubble Space Telescope is supposed to be the most important advance in astronomy since Galileo looked through his modest prototype four centuries ago.

Hubble died in 1953, but more than 100 of his kinfolk came here for the scheduled launch.

But a rookie writer on the space beat couldn't help but note the fact that five humans were to man the shuttle that sat Monday afternoon on the same pad where seven Americans rocketed into immortality in January 1986. The names of the five: Loren Shriver, Charles Bolden Jr., Bruce McCandless II, Steve Hawley and Kathryn Sullivan, the youngest being 39, the oldest 53.

And a rookie couldn't help but notice a shuttle launch is still an event down here where businesses show their support with cheerleader signs and American flags.

Monday afternoon, rows of Port-o-let toilets already were in place to accommodate the masses expected to jam the causeway leading to Kennedy Space Center for the launch.

Monday night, innkeepers told tourists who didn't have coveted badges that got them close enough that they should leave early, find Highway 1, follow it until they saw the crowd and watch from across the water.

Hotels and motels were booked solid and press credentials had been issued to more reporters and photographers than anybody could remember recently.

One of NASA's press bus drivers, an old veteran of launches dating back to the Apollo moon missions, stood on the steps of his bus and said, "It is always exciting."

Discovery was bright and alive in the lights on Pad 39-B. A full moon hung over the ocean. It was an awesome sight.

(April 10, 1990)

Golf As a Scale Model of the Way Life's Lived

What I like about golf is not being out in the fresh air and getting a little exercise from walking the course. What I like about the game is it's a scale model of the way life is lived.

Golf's rules are designed to reveal the character traits of those playing it, and you can find out much about yourself - and about others - when it comes to playing golf by the letter of the law. For example, many players invoke what are called "winter rules" when they play, even if it's in the middle of hot July.

"Winter rules" mean a player uses his club to roll the ball over on the grass of the fairway so there will always be a preferred lie. Many use this rule even when they're in the rough.

However, there's no such thing as "winter rules" in the rules of golf. The basic nature of the game is you play the ball as it lies. Only under certain stringent conditions can the ball be moved from where it comes to rest after being hit, and those conditions are unequivocally pointed out in the rules.

When an errant drive lands amid the roots of a

spreading chestnut tree, it's tempting to nudge the ball into a position from where the next shot will be easier to play.

And why not?

Although usually played in groups, golf's really a solitary game with many opportunities to remove your ball from hateful positions while other members of your group are looking for theirs. When I've observed fellow competitors breaching these rules, I've often wondered whether they take advantage of the basic rules in life, too.

Until I realized years ago that the game of golf is a mirror in which a man can see his soul, I'd casually roll the ball onto a better lie on the fairway grass, too. My enjoyment of the game multiplied once I decided to obey its tenets and play the ball and the course as I found them, which is how the book of rules says each must be played.

In other words, if the course is a little wet and your drive lands in a soggy spot not considered "casual water" as described in the book, you must play the ball where it lies. If you move it, you're cheating the game, cheating your playing companions and, most of all, cheating yourself.

How many of us move the ball on the golf course of life? Society has basic rules just as the game of golf does: We're expected to obey speed limits; penalties will be imposed if we're caught cheating on tax returns; jail awaits those caught stealing, et cetera.

I hope most people obey these basic rules, or else America's in more trouble than a golfer whose ball is buried under the lip of a sand bunker. Golfers often don't count every stroke they take; citizens often don't report all the money they make. Golfers sometimes use illegal equipment; businesses sometimes use illegal methods.

You can learn lots about yourself by playing golf, but if you're not real careful, a good deal of it won't be very flattering.

(July 22, 1997)

She Always Made It Fun and Better

She was always the one who did extra things to make life a little easier and a lot more fun. She still does, in her modest, caring way, for she grew up in a time when people had to stand together and help each other, and she never lost the trait.

I remember being read to by lamplight, and even then I understood she had unlocked a door through which I could enter into a room filled with a lifetime of pleasure. I thank her for making me a reader of books.

She would have taken in every stray dog and cat if she could have had her way. But he wouldn't let her, for it was all he could do to feed three sons, a wife, and himself. Yet she never chased a hungry animal away from her kitchen door until she slipped it something to eat. I learned names of trees and flowers from her, and in the process discovered the true contentment of a simple walk through the woods or down a country road.

She taught me that a glass is half-full, not half empty, that a day is partly sunny, not partly cloudy, and that a smile, even if it's forced, can disarm the enemy.

If I lied, she whipped me. If I erred but told the truth no matter how it hurt, she explained what she expected. The foolishness she tolerated, but not the lies.

When my friends wanted to hitchhike to town to see a picture show and I didn't have the quarter, she gave it to me from the milk money he left her. Then she faced him down when he raised Cain about it. It happened a number of times.

Jeans were always patched. Shirts were always ironed. Holes in the toes of socks were always sewn. When they went to town on Saturday to buy groceries, she always managed to slip a sack of cookies into the bag when he had his head turned or was down another aisle.

They were as different as daylight and dark. He was fiery, tempermental and mean as a snake when cornered. She was calm, even-keeled and as sweet as fine-grained sugar. And still is.

Pink is her favorite color. She likes to watch golf on television because of all the flowers, trees, water and green grass on the courses.

She never had a daughter, and wanted one real bad, and there was a span of time after her first granddaughter was born when she literally begged the parents to let her have the little girl. She told the parents they were young and could have another, and she was as serious as the day is long. She finally settled for just keeping it with her -- sometimes for a week. Today, right now, she stills feels deep in her heart the girl is her daughter.

When he died, she moved to town, and for a

long time, until arthritis and age began to have their way, she grew roses and tomatoes, and probably would have had some chickens in her yard if she'd been able to get away with it. She has lived through most of this century, and has greeted each new technological discovery with child-like delight.

She cries sadly when the Bakkers and Swaggarts disgrace themselves. She laughs happily when good fortune comes to one of her family members. She never has wished a bad thing on anyone or harmed a single person in her life. And hers has been a long and eventful life, filled with sorrow and joy, but she never talks about sadness, only happiness.

Millions like her have come and gone, millions like her are with us today, and those of us who've been in their presence are better humans because of them.

To her and to them: Happy Mother's Day.

(May 13, 1990)

Looking for Hushbone
on the Figure Out Channel

Life was going to be much simpler the closer I got to the rocking chair. Having scaled the mountain of make-believe and gotten the silly stuff behind me, it looked like a downhill slide all the way to greener pastures. But just when I thought I knew all I needed to know, I've had to start learning all over again.

Tired of the same old outlook? Fed up with hearing the same old questions and answers from your equally fed-up friends? Start hanging with the 4-year-olds and your attitude is bound to change.

I don't care what all you've seen and heard or how jaded your heart is, you can learn a lot from children - especially pre-schoolers who still look at the world through innocent eyes. For example, one of my 4-year-old pals wanted to watch a certain television program while he was visiting me the other night. What channel is it on? I asked.

"Put it on the figure out channel," he said, "and you can find it."

The figure out channel?

"You know," he replied, "the one that has all

the programs so you can figure out which ones to watch."

How could I have been so dumb? He wanted the television guide channel that scrolls programs being shown that night. You know, the figure out channel.

This is the fellow who once asked whether I liked to watch Hushbone. Additional interrogation revealed Hushbone is actually Wishbone, the little dog on Public Television who pretends to be famous people.I watched one afternoon with my pal, and the dog did look like a Hushbone to me.

It also hasn't taken long for my other 4-year-old pal to teach me about language (and reasoning). I was mystified when she asked whether she could have "sour" to drink with her dinner until she took me to the refrigerator and pointed to a can of Sprite.

Yep, confirmed her parents, "sour" is what she calls soft drinks such as Sprite, Seven-Up and Mountain Dew - probably because the tart taste is sour to her.

I had forgotten what a great actor Barney Rubble is until I started hanging out with 4-year-olds again. Barney is to Fred Flintstone what Gracie was to George Burns, what Norton was to Ralph Cramden and what crackers are to Vienna sausage.

Socializing with 4-year-old people has also made me realize just how much the little children depend on the big people. They trust us to keep them warm when they're cold, to provide food for them when they're hungry and to make sure there are no monsters under the bed when they're ready to go to sleep.

Being trusted by them is an awesome and humbling responsibility; any man or woman who would break that trust and ignore the responsibility most surely is in danger of hell's fire.

So I have begun to learn anew. Scrunched up on the couch with one of my pals, a glass of sour in one hand, the remote control in the other, I scan the figure out channel looking for something to watch.

Most anything will do. I've already been enlightened.

(February 16, 1999)

41

II. Looking Back

Of Paupers and Passion and Paradise

NEW MARKET -- On the first day of October the sun rolled like a gold wheel across a clear blue sky, and I didn't dream I'd be reminded of the poor on such a rich day.

But on a sparkling Tuesday with temperatures more summer than fall I stood on an extraordinary spot and saw for the first time in my life that pauper's graves are real.

In the ground beneath towering oaks on a grassy hill in a pasture near here was evidence.

Rows of depressions in the earth marked final resting places of God only knows how many of His children who went to heaven without us knowing their names.

There's a public park near this place now. Livestock grazes in the field. To get there you must go down a rutted lane and open a gate which keeps cows in.

It's a quiet, lonely, remote place which almost nobody knows and where hardly anybody goes.

Just the kind of place to hide society's skeletons.

If there hadn't been a landfill flap out here, bones buried on the hillside and in an oak grove a few hundred yards east would have stayed forgotten, footnotes only in "A Dream Come True." New Market son James Record's history of Madison County.

But a passionate uprising over garbage dump land led New Market to uncover part of its history. Newcomers should be aware. New Market is pedigreed. It was settled in 1806, a year before John Hunt camped at Big Spring in what's now downtown Huntsville

They learned this cemetery, the graveyard without tombstones, was on some of the proposed landfill.

Well, that wouldn't do. They lobbied the Alabama Historic Register. It was saved in 1990.,

Saturday Oct. 19, a plaque will be erected to commemorate the place, tours of the site and historic New Market homes will be conducted, and a barbeque supper will be served at Sharon Johnston Park -- which you can read about in the regular news columns closer to the event. I'm sure.

But what about being reminded about the poor on a rich day.

The spot where I stood Tuesday had a name. A somber, bleak name to us in the late 20th century. In those days (1870 to 1923) people weren't as sensitive about what they called each other.

Where big oaks now stand and unmarked graves now lay was once the Madison County Poorhouse and Cemetery for the "indigent, lame, and unfortunate.

As late as 1935 there were 63 "poorhouses" in the state. From 1923 to 1935 one was located at the end of Hermitage Street in Huntsville at the foot of Monte Sano mountain. It was called the Almshouse.

Poorhouse, Almshouse, whatever, they were for people without homes, which shows homelessness in Madison County isn't a recent thing.

The poorhouse at New Market lasted 53 years, and James Record's history quotes residents remembering pine coffins being hauled to it on wagons down Goodner Road, , nicknamed Poorhouse Road, which is now Beth Road.

Men, women, children and babies, indigent and lame, black and white, buried nameless in those pine coffins, paupers buried in pauper's graves.

I looked at the graves in that pasture and thought about mental illness, crippling disease and injury, poverty, and apathy.

Maybe it's good to be reminded of such things on days sent from paradise.

(October 3, 1991)

Rejoicing on a Day God Made

SOLITUDE -- Robert O. Johnson, that Marshall County landmark with a camera around his neck, directed from the bed of Tom Jordan's pickup.

"Older people in the chairs, children on the ground in front, the rest line up behind, and everybody smile." He banged on the cab and got Tom moving toward the road so everybody would be in the picture. There being a dip in Solitude Road just before the rise where shutterbug Johnson wanted him, Tom moved slow, cautious about getting T-boned by somebody cresting the hill.

This was Sunday when congregation and visitors posed for a historic photograph in front of a historic place. Solitude Baptist Church, organized in 1891, was once the largest rural Baptist church in Marshall County. It was called Union Baptist in September, 1891, when services began in a log school on Solitude Road. Two months later members paid William Wyatt $4 for 2 1/2 acres, and Solitude Baptist had a permanent home.

Powerful preachers have stood in Solitude's pulpit, and the church long ago became a leader in mission outreach. It helped start two other churches in Marshall County and one in Montana, and several of its congregation became distinguished Southern Baptist missionaries.

One is Clarabelle McDonald, who was Clarabelle Isdell before she married Homer McDonald. Before marrying, Clarabelle was a missionary to China and Hawaii. Her father, R.L. Isdell, and brother, E.J. Isdell, both pastored Solitude.

Clarabelle once did a history of the church. Now 89, she was among those posing for Sunday's picture. The picture will appear in an updated centennial version of her history. But the real reason a big crowd came Sunday was it was both homecoming and decoration day.

Chalmus Couch, who said "several things has got its drawbacks" about being 77 years old, sat on the tailgate of a pickup under a shade tree and watched people lay flowers on graves. As chairman of the cemetery committee, Deacon Couch kept an eye on that most hallowed of rural Southern Baptist church traditions, in case somebody had questions about grave sites. But his mind was on the food waiting to be served after morning worship services.

"I can't get nobody to bring sweet tater cobbler," he said with an impish smile.

Everybody at Solitude is friendly, beginning with Pastor Willis Kelly, a slender man who has preached in this old country church for 19 years while his wife Mary has sung in the choir. "Now make yourself at home," was his first commandment after shaking hands.

He didn't preach a full sermon but turned homecoming over to members and former members who testified about love and happiness and taking care of each other, things Christian people everywhere say, but especially in rural churches. Seven children sang "this is the day the Lord hath made; I will rejoice and be glad in it." Young voices, old voices, high voices and low voices blended as a choir of 17 adults sang "Amazing Grace."

Then Robert Johnson made his picture and everybody went to dinner, which is what a noon meal's still called here, and which, with or without sweet potato cobbler, was heavenly.

(May 19, 1992)

Life Remains the Same on Main Street

MADISON -- It's in the middle of one of the fastest growing areas in the Western Hemisphere, but nothing much has changed on Main Street in the last 50 years. In fact, downtown Madison "looks the same" to E.J. `'Gene" Anderson as it did in 1946 when he got out of the Army Air Corps and began running his father-in-law's hardware store.

About the only difference is there's a radio station in G. Walton Hughes' old drug store. Everything else, including Hughes Hardware, which Gene Anderson operates with his youngest son Walt, looks like it did when Madison was a thriving country town at the outbreak of World War II.

There were three cotton gins in Madison in 1940. The town was situated on one-half square mile. The population was 430. The gins are gone, but Madison's still a thriving town with a mixture of country heritage and space age technology whose tax base is built on a firm foundation of commercial and residential growth unlike many other places in America.

The small hamlet in western Madison County has grown from 430 people to a population of about 20,000, and Gene Anderson has seen it all through the windows of Hughes Hardware. In 1942, Gene married Marion Hughes in January and was drafted in February. Sensing war and expecting a shortage of farm equipment, Walton Hughes, Marion's father, bought the stock of a Madison hardware store at a bankruptcy ale. During the war, Mr. Hughes would keep the store closed until customers came to him at his drug store next door asking to be let in.

The second day the Andersons were back on Main Street after the war, Walton Hughes gave Gene the keys to the hardware store and told him to run it. He has ever since, from 7 a.m. until 5:30 p.m. six days a week, unless he and Marion take time off to travel.

In the 1950s, Anderson and other farsighted Madisonians realized they needed to get busy "or else Huntsville would have surrounded us long before now." He ran for mayor and was elected, serving with Joe Balch and Gordon Hughes in the commission form of government Madison had then. He feels their service "set the base for what's happening now."

Although Madison changed from a village with $8,000 "total income" for a year to a town that recently passed an annual budget of $7.1 million, Gene Anderson, like Main Street, remains consistent: husband to the same woman for 52 years, father of two sons, Larry and Walt, grandfather of six, and a man who still greets customers from the front counter of his hardware store.

His past is represented by black-and-white framed photos in his office of wagon loads of cotton waiting to be ginned at one of Madison's three gins. His present is expressed by a Macintosh computer beside his desk. His future is symbolized by pictures of his sons and their wives and children.

Does he feel good about life? "I've really been happy," Gene Anderson said with a nod of his head and a satisfied smile.

(November 3, 1994)

Some Things Won't Easily Tear Down

That big March snow caused the roof to collapse, so the owner tore the rest down. Now there's just a bare spot where Carroll's Grocery stood. But if I live to be 100, every time I drive past where it was I'll think about the two people who ran it.

Their names were Bill and Christine Thigpen. She was a daughter of the original owners and he was a boy who worked there. Together they became parents of a large family and friends of an entire community. Of the 11 Thigpen children, eight survive. One of them is the mother of my children. I consider the others my friends.

But long before I met them, Christine and Bill Thigpen were known as two of the Dallas Mill village and Northeast Huntsville's most solid citizens. There was, literally, nothing they wouldn't do for anybody. When times were tough for everybody, or when times were tough for individuals, Carroll's Grocery would "carry" you. When Bill Thigpen died, his children found a thick stack of unpaid bills, most of them yellowed with age, in the drawers of an old desk where the cash register sat. If you could pay them, OK, but if you couldn't, that was OK, too.

Bll and Christine possessed two of the sweetest dispositions God ever gave a man and a woman. I once asked if any of the children ever heard either of their parents raise a voice in anger. Not a one said they had. My love for the two of them was, and is, no secret, and after my own father's death, Bill Thigpen became my father figure. There was an unspoken bond between us I always enjoyed. On the day he died, I cried as hard as I ever cried in my life, refusing, in my selfish immaturity, to accept the fact he, too, had left me.

Sometimes when I open the door of my memory, he's either loading groceries into his old green-panel delivery truck or cutting meat on his bloodied-up, nicked-up chopping block. I see him clearly: short, lean, wavy haired, apron tied around his little waist, a contented smile always on his lips. If he wasn't delivering or in the store, you'd find him next door at Eunice Merrell's cafe drinking coffee.

J.D. and Flossie Carroll started their store in 1913 on Oakwood Avenue. Friends ran it for him when he went off to World War II. In the mid-1920s, J.D. and Flossie built a new store on Fifth Street, which eventually became Andrew Jackson Way.

Bill Thigpen married Christine Carroll, then

operated the store after J.D. died. He and his wife ran it with Christian kindness and human goodness, like they ran their lives. Nobody who knew them will ever say anything bad about them.

Bill and Christine taught us all some important lessons in that little brick-and-board grocery store across from the Baptist church on Andrew Jackson Way.

We learned, not from words, but from actions, that it is truly more blessed to give than to receive. We learned that if the meek don't inherit the Earth, they most assuredly will own heaven. Maybe most of all, we learned that greatness doesn't belong only to those with wealth and power.

So there's no more Carroll's Grocery now. But Bill and Christine Thigpen haven't gone anywhere. They'll always be here in my heart.

(May 18, 1993)

In a Setting of Solitude
and Pioneers

JONES HOLLOW -- Bill and Anne Jones live at
the spot on Upper Hurricane Road where asphalt
ends and gravel begins, but theirs is not the last
house on this highway. If you're eager, and if your
vehicle has rear-wheel drive at least, you can
follow the sparse track up to Sawmill Hollow,
where the mighty Hurricane Creek begins, and
pass dwellings of other pioneer-types on the way.

Bill Jones truly comes from pioneers.
Somewhere between 1816 and 1818, young
Seburn Jones got a land grant and became squire
of hundreds of acres of prime bottom land and
wooded mountains in northeastern Madison
County. As the 20th century ends, Bill and Anne
live on 600 acres of Seburn's land in the hollow
that bears the family name.

Fom her kitchen window, Anne can see one of
two original Jones family cabins off in the distance
up the hollow. It was built somewhere around
1850 for one of Seburn's sons, Thomas, and his
wife, Rachel. It was added to twice, and until 1952
was the official residence of Bill's parents, William

Rob and Jessie Florence Jones, and their 11 children.

Bill was one of the first five men in Madison County drafted for World War II. He drove a tank in Patton's Third Army. Part of his outfit helped capture Berlin. Anne stayed some with Rob and Jessie in the historical old place while Bill was off fighting in Germany, and she has fond memories of an outhouse, which, like most of the main house, remains.The trunk of a giant beech tree partially hides the front of the house. Peach and pear trees behind it still bear fruit. Hurricane Creek runs down a rocky bed yards from the porch. The creek in front of the house is easy to ford most times, even after heavy rains, for water runs off swiftly here at its upper level.

Bill Jones, 79, built a gazebo around a well in the yard. Until a third stroke sidelined him in November, he and Anne often went there on late afternoons and she'd read the newspaper while he'd watch for deer. They intend for him to grow strong enough to do that again.

Anne Jones, nimble and witty at 71, president of the New Market Homemakers Club which she helped organize, was born on Gurley Mountain. She met Bill at Hurricane Grove Baptist Church. They married Aug. 1, 1942, and have two sons, Bill Jones Jr., who works at the post office, and Robert Jones, who owns his own business in Georgia, and six grandchildren.

Bill and Anne became farmers because none of Bill's seven brothers or three sisters wanted the place. They bought it in 1955, after living 10 years in Florida, where Bill was a brick mason, because he couldn't find work here. Ironically, old Seburn himself, the fountainhead who fathered 19 children with two wives, Polly first, then Eleanor, before dying in 1867, was a stone mason by trade who cut many of the rocks used to mark graves in the family cemetery on the forested hill behind his son's cabin.

Now framed by redbud and wildflowers, washed by the clear, rushing water of Hurricane Creek, and almost forgotten except by those who live here, Jones Hollow is one of the last great secluded sites in Madison County.

For Bill and Anne Jones, however, the silence of solitude is a splendid reminder of the roots from which he sprang and of the heritage both of them are obliged to abide. To be sure, they are proud stewards of Thomas Jones' historic cabin and Seburn Jones' ancient land.

(March 31, 1994)

In a Valley Whose Views
Still Please the Curious

PRINCETON -- The hay's already in the barns and the living's easy out where Alabama 65 twists through Paint Rock Valley on its way to Tennessee. But as nearby mountains shimmer like mirages in the hot afternoon sun, it's hard to remember hay is winter feed that helps cattle survive cold weather when there's no grass for grazing.

Most sightseers like to make this drive in springtime when wild flowers are blooming or in autumn when leaves are changing, but August's as good a month and summer's as fine a season as any. From its origin on U.S. 72 East in Jackson County to where it changes numbers at the Tennessee line, state road 65 remains one of the most scenic drives in the area.

The route got its first fame because it passed two historic places: Paint Rock Valley High School here and the Walls of Jericho down the road. Built as a post-Depression effort by the Works Progress Administration, the original school buildings are constructed of rock hauled from a hill behind the school.

Kitty Henshaw, 92, known to Princetonians as "our historical society," said children helped workers load rocks in wagons, which were pulled to the building site by mules. Mrs. Henshaw and her late husband, Oscar, sent four children to Paint Rock Valley High School, which remains the main focus for valley families who also live in places like Trenton and Hollytree.

God built the Walls of Jericho at the dawn of time, and the majesty of this huge rock face on the side of a mountain has drawn many professional climbers, amateur explorers and tourists. Mrs. Henshaw remembered going there in a wagon with a Sunday School class. She recalled it being "a bumpy ride." Hoping to make it a major tourist attraction, private enterprise later bought the site and built something of a road.

While the Walls of Jericho is still there, the dream's not, and access is supposedly discouraged by barriers built to keep the curious from hurting themselves. Still, Alabama 65 has enough history and scenery to encourage a couple of travelers with time on their hands to use it as a short cut on a return trip from southern Tennessee.

On this day:

--Church houses with names like Hall's Chapel, Holly Grove and Mt. Nebo waited quietly beside the road for Wednesday prayer meetings and Sunday preaching services.

--A man holding a dog in his lap sat in a lawn chair placed in a shallow creek while three children splashed in the rusty water around him.

--Corn and soybeans grew in emerald fields that stretched to the feet of surrounding mountains.

--Valley residents driving pickup trucks and cars or working in yards waved at passing strangers, a ritual in which city dwellers hardly ever engage.

All this took place on a hot day when two inquisitive deer were also seen standing by the side of the winding road that runs through Paint Rock Valley.

(August 7, 1997)

The Proof Is in the Life He Lived

During those infrequent periods when I call myself exercising, long neighborhood walks always make juices flow and joints jangle. Many of the reasons are aesthetic, from beds of azaleas blooming in springtime to leaves changing color in fall.

The trail leads up busy boulevards and down quiet streets, and one particular leg of the stroll has always been livened by the prospect of maybe seeing a legend. You don't get to see one every day, you know, but in good weather chances for a sighting were better than average. He might have been on the porch reading a newspaper and smoking a cigar. He might have been working in the yard and smoking a cigar. Or he might have just been doing nothing and smoking a cigar.

Whatever he was doing, he always had a friendly wave or a comment about something on his mind, whether he recognized you or not. Recognizing you wasn't a factor, anyway, because he knew if he didn't know you, you knew him. That's how people get to be legends? Anyway, part of the fun of the walk was wondering whether or not he'd be outside when I reached his house.

Well, that part of those walks won't be quite as much fun now. Cecil Fain died Monday at age 96. He sure handled being a legend well for a long time. But, then, he always handled things with a gentlemanly grace and a Southern dignity that set him apart from the herd.

Cecil Fain was many things, but most of all he was a school teacher. He was a principal and an administrator and all that other stuff. But in the deepest recesses of his kind and generous heart, he was a school teacher. There'll be many Cecil Fain stories dusted off and recycled by the time he's buried Thursday, and if you don't think they're all true, well, act like it, anyway, because he'll be tickled.

He didn't do much: started the first student safety patrol, was principal of eight schools, coached every sport, brought tennis to Huntsville, taught Sunday school for 60 years, organized the county's first PTA group, first Boy Scout troop, first American Legion post ... and taught God knows how many boys and girls how to be men and women.

One time some of us slipped across Oakwood Avenue at noon to eat at Mullins. Just when our bowls of chili, oyster crackers and soft drinks were delivered, he walked in. He made us pay, then herded us like cattle back across Oakwood to Rison School, hungry, defeated and a whole lot wiser than when we started.

Paul Anderson remembers Cecil Fain as being a great competitor, whether it was in a classroom or on a tennis court.

"We were playing Florence in one of those independent league matches one day, and Fain was paired against a college kid," Anderson said. "How old was Fain? He was about 60. He's always been 60, I reckon. Fain hurt himself, but to show you how his mind clicked, he wanted to put a sub in to finish the match so we wouldn't lose the point.

"Of course, Florence wouldn't hear of that. But that's the way he was. He hated losing."

Cecil Fain never lost too many, in anything. The proof of that is how he lived his life, the positive things he accomplished and the many true friends he made along the way.

(January 29, 1992)

A Monument to "Family"
Is Unveiled

Woodrow Dunn said this about the men and women he supervised: "I don't think anybody anywhere worked harder than the people of this mill." He said it Sunday, but his opinion was formed years ago when he was superintendent of Huntsville Manufacturing Co. The big plant on Triana Boulevard closed in 1991, the last Huntsville textile giant to bite the dust.

Dallas was turned into a shoe manufacturing company and then sat empty for years before it burned. Lincoln burned, too, after it closed, but part of it still stands, reminding those who live around it of past glory. Now the one on Triana's coming down, the one called Merrimack when it was built in 1899.

Sunday, in sight of the tall smokestack still standing, a hundred or so people met at Brahan Springs Park to dedicate a monument to Merrimack mill and village and to Joe Bradley School. Shaped like a pyramid, the memorial sits on a base built from bricks taken from the old mill's remains.

Murphy Stolz, one of three generations of

Merrimackers, designed the simple, attractive memorial. On its sides are pictures of mill, school and company stores. There are also 520 names of people who worked in the mill, lived in the village or attended the school. Either them or their relatives paid $25 to have those names placed on the plaque, and Bill Gant, chairman of the committee which put together the Merrimack/Joe Bradley monument, said he expects another 200 to apply.

Merrimack and Joe Bradley people donated $8,000 to the project, Councilman Bill Kling helped get city approval, and several others freely gave time and material for construction. E.F. Dubose, who was principal of Bradley school from 1923 until 1967, and Helen Krivutza, who as Helen Young received the last diploma Joe Bradley High School gave, helped unveil the monument.

Merrimack Manufacturing Co. built the mill, the village and a school. Shifts were 12 hours and wages were $3 to $4 per week in 1900. Children went to school half a day and worked in the mill half a day. M. L. Lowenstein bought the mill in 1946, changed its name to Huntsville Manufacturing Co., and called the village Huntsville Park.

There are still 67 families living in what is considered the village, the oldest person there being Arthur Boyington Sr., about to be 95. At Sunday's unveiling, much applause met the committee's suggestion that it will try to get the name Merrimack returned to the village. Kling and Mayor Steve Hettinger said they thought that should happen, and Hettinger, in his remarks, called the unveiling "truly a great day in our community's history. Huntsville's work ethic and sense of pride in community was founded on the mill villages. You are what Huntsville is about," he said.

Master of ceremonies and former Madison County Sheriff Jerry Crabtree, who grew up in Merrimack, said it was fitting "to dedicate a monument to all who lived there, worked there and went to school there so all who come along later will know we were here."

Mill Superintendent Dunn probably captured best the spirit of the people whose names are on the marker when he said, "If there ever was a family, the people of Joe Bradley and Huntsville Park are family."

(July 15, 1992)

By Any Name He's Still
a History Book

KRAMER HOLLOW -- Fred Baker, who'd rather be called Bill, tells this story about one of his ancestors, Uncle Jess Edwards: Fox hunting was a local passion in the late 1800s, and nobody loved it more than Uncle Jess. Problem was he was a commoner while the other hunters were upper crust. However, it was a problem for the snobs, not for Jess. When the landed gentry gathered in red coats and polished boots to ride to hounds on handsome, coiffured horses, likely as not Uncle Jess joined them.

Only he wore overalls and rode an old gray mule. What a colorful image: Spit and polish glinting in the sun, a flamboyant company of hunters sweeps down the cove, their loud, lusty yells mingling with the barking of the hounds; in their midst rides the startling figure of Jess, waving his hat, overall strap flapping, whooping and hollering with all his might, the old gray mule braying loudly and twirling its tail around and around in the air in excitement. "That kind of knocked the shine off the party," Bill Baker said, his weather-beaten face wearing a satisfied grin. The reason he's called Bill is, "For some reason I didn't like the name Fred, so Pa started calling me Bill."

It's Fred Baker on the battered mailbox marking the little gravel-and-dirt road leading to where he lives on Upper Hurricane Road with his wife of 47 years, Jessie Jacks Baker. But everybody around New Market calls him Bill.

William Baker, who married Hannah Edwards and had six children, was the first Baker here. According to carvings on his grave stone, William showed up from Guilford County, N.C., in 1807. He died in the 1860s and is buried in the Baker family cemetery beneath a grove of trees atop a hill down the road apiece from Bill's and Jessie's house.

The Bakers live in Kramer Hollow because a Canadian named Fred Kramer originally lived on 20 acres at the head of the cove. Nobody knows why Kramer ended up in Madison County in the 1800s, but it's documented that he married a local girl, Elizabeth Sharp, and stayed.

When Bill Baker got out of the Army Air Corps in 1945 and started back from the war in the Pacific, he was on a Cherokee Line bus when it made a stop in Huntsville and a girl named Jessie Jacks, going home to Plevna, got on. His memory was of "a little gal running around in pigtails" when he had last seen her, but Jessie said it wasn't pigtails, it was bangs.Whatever, Jessie said they "kind of liked each other" when they met again on the bus. They married two years later. Now they have four sons, Pete, Jack, Jeff and David, and five grandchildren with "one on the way."

Jessie said "I was kind of lonely at first" about being stuck off in Kramer Hollow. But as the years passed, "I got so I liked to be by myself." A panoramic look of the beautiful hollow where she lives is enough to make a stranger understand how she beat being lonely.

Fred Baker, called Bill, runs livestock on his pastures but does not row crop now. He retired from NASA in 1980 and spends much of his time piddling with machinery on his place and watching his grandchildren grow.

He also has become a historian, one of those priceless people who should be encouraged at every opportunity, for without the Bill Bakers of this world none of us would ever get to imagine a whooping Uncle Jess Edwards riding to hounds astride a braying old gray mule.

(April 1, 1994)

III. Notable People

The Only Link Left in the Chain

The service had started when an old black man whose legs were bowed by the weight of his years and an awful case of the gout shambled across the rain-soaked, mud-caked ground to a seat beneath the funeral tent.

Sacred songs had been sung and kind words had been spoken when he arrived, and helpful hands reached out to guide him each painful step of his way across a slick slope to where the casket lay.

It had stopped raining, but the trip was still dangerous for an old man with a bent back and gimpy legs. There was no keeping him away, though, for he was always there when the man whose body was in the polished wooden box needed him. On this day, with the sky full of dark, cheerless clouds, John Fleming felt his friend needed him more than ever.

John, his brother Ivy Fleming, and Waddy Lowe were boys whose fathers worked for Aaron Fleming, who owned a lot of land along

Whitesburg Drive all the way to the Tennessee River.

John, Ivy and Waddy became playmates with Aaron Fleming's sons. When Aaron died and the sons assumed control of the land, the three young friends also succeeded their fathers and went to work on the Fleming farm.

As the years passed, John Fleming, the black employee, became best friends with Walton Fleming, the white landowner. They shared a mutual trust and a genuine love. They were tied together by such a bond of friendship, it could only be broken by death.

Walton Fleming was one of those rare people who truly saw past the color of skin. He was more interested in things like character, dignity and loyalty. The large crowd that came on the dreary day that was Friday to see his body buried in the ground and his soul committed to heaven was a testament to the kind of life he lived.

What his powerful influence meant to the past, present and future of Huntsville and how his philanthropy made it possible for many individuals and organizations to survive have been thoroughly documented.

What hasn't been said is the best thing about him was he was so interested in what was happening in the lives of his children, their children and their children, it bordered on meddling.

Every one of them forgave him for it, though, and loved him dearly. "My only prayer is my kids grow up to be like him," said one of his daughters, Gay Fleming Parker, who had to rush home from China when told of her father's death. "He was the kind of man I wish I could be," declared his son, Pete Fleming.

And old John Fleming, who listened to the service with his head bowed while tears the size of rain drops rolled down his cheeks, knows he is the last link in what was a magnificent chain, and when he goes, so goes an era.

(January 26, 1997)

His Legacy Was a Life of Goodness

Fay Samples had a simple request when asked what would make him comfortable.

"I heard Chet Atkins play "Stardust" on television once, and I sure would like to hear him play it again."

But it looked like a dead end street when it was found Atkins never recorded Hoagy Carmichael's hit.

Then family friend Dan Aldrich called Atkins' publisher in Nashville and explained the dilemma. The publisher told the famed guitarist. Atkins bought a blank tape, took it to a studio, paid musicians to back him up, recorded the song, sent it and a letter.

So for a few days Fay Samples, guitarist and pianist in his own right, was the only person in the world who owned a recording of Stardust by Chet Atkins.

Being the only one of a kind never bothered Fay. That's why when Beatrice, his wife, once told him to get rid of a broken tree limb hanging in their front yard he simply shot it down with a shotgun.

Recently a chaplain, making small talk, asked

Fay if he ever had a garden. "No, I'm kinda lazy," was the answer. "But my neighbor has one, and he gives me things."

Neighbor Bob Culley is one of many people who gladly shared with Fay, and a multitude of them were at the funeral home last night telling stories.

Fay Alexander Samples, 80, died Saturday night. He fought cancer for over two years. He fought well until the last month.

He was born in Ennis, Tex. as the son of a dentist who moved much, including stops on Sand Mountain and in New Hope.

Orville Samples died when Fay was 14, and the boy went to live with relatives in Huntsville. He got a job in the Dallas Mill when he was 16, left there to help build Redstone Arsenal, moved on to Denver, and ended up in Alaska working on a pipeline. He inherited more than a little of his daddy's wanderlust.

After family and friends, he loved music. It didn't take much push for him to play piano and sing. Sandra Bentley, his daughter, said he spent the last few weeks of his life humming and singing "That Lucky Old Sun."

It's easy to see him rolling around heaven all day doing nothing but making people happy.

Which is what he did best. "I've never seen a more un-materialistic man," said his son, Ty. "His grandchildren didn't go to him and ask him for a dollar, they went to him and asked him about life."

Beatrice and Fay Samples were married 56 years, and she knew him best of all. She said his worth was head and shoulders above anything else he might have been.

"He was a very good man," she said. "He was a good father and a good husband. He loved people and they loved him, and you can tell that by how many came to see him."

Many remembrances of the man who hardly ever met a stranger flowed Monday night, and the best, of course, came from his children, their children, and theirs.

All the stories told by Fay's old pals who sat with him on benches in Parkway City Mall most days to watch the world were also a celebration of his life.

But Beatrice had the best perspective of all when asked to sum up her husband. "It was a full life," she said. "A merry-go-round."

Then she added what could easily be carved on his stone: "He was kind and good to everyone."

(July 28, 1992)

74

Humaneness on a Scale Unheard Of

If a man's worth is judged by good works, William Cooper Green Jr. was a billionaire.

I've never known a person so wrapped up in both his own affairs and those of his community. We who worked with him often wondered how he found time to run two of Alabama's major daily newspapers and still sit on all those volunteer boards and devote all that time to charity.

Bill Green was more than just publisher of *The Huntsville Times* and *The Huntsville News*. He was a pillar of the city, a steward of the county and a fresh breath of hope for the Tennessee Valley. His death Wednesday leaves a tear in the fabric of this area which can't easily be stitched.

Obituaries in both papers documented his record of service to mankind, and an awesome record it was. Because of him, many service and civic organizations enjoyed not only free publicity courtesy of community service advertisements, they also enjoyed his presence on their boards.

And a rather outgoing presence it was. Bill Green was of average height, but there was nothing else average about him. Thick, wavy hair, which had started turning the color of prime cotton, made him look like a statesman. He also had a foghorn voice which sounded like a tuba in a marching band. That made any kind of confidential talk with him hard to conduct.

But, then, he was a man who didn't talk about people behind their backs, so there was no need for a governor to be put on those magnificent vocal chords.

None who worked for him ever heard that voice raised in anger. His approach to dealing with us was soft and gentle. But his determination in all matters was such it was easy to understand exactly what was being said and what was to be expected.

His kind is called a leader, and you don't get to be one without being born with certain qualities.

Bill Green's biggest quality was his humaneness. Being chief executive of the area's highest-profile industry could turn many men into power-hungry, overbearing aristocrats intent on promoting themselves. But his total lack of selfishness was such a dramatic reversal of form that each of his employees felt he was their friend.

Except on rare occasions when he shared top-secret information with other Times and News executives, the door to Bill Green's office was never closed.

For a fact, he often brought it up at staff meetings or put letters in pay envelopes inviting us to come talk over our problems with him.

76

One of the lasting images I'll have of him is seeing him thumb through his jam-packed daily calendar trying to find another hour in any particular day to do something else someone wanted done.

In the last months of his life, when he was sick and probably should have been in bed, he would have Janie, his wife, drive him to work so he could sit behind his desk and conduct business.

I don't know what drove Bill Green from way before daylight to way past dark but I do know the result of his marathon lifestyle was a better world for both those who worked for him and those who never knew him.

He was blessed, too, in having a family that understood and supported his passionate need to contribute more than his share.

William Cooper Green Jr., dead at age 72, also had a multitude of friends and admirers who will miss his beaming smile, his booming voice and his boisterous personality.

(May 13, 1994)

An Impact of Matchless Proportions

Strangers wouldn't have any way of knowing, but even some who've lived here long enough to be called natives might not understand Louis Salmon's impact on this community.

His obituary in the newspapers indicated what a busy life he lived: a list of civic endeavors and personal achievements as long as your arm.

But who, really, was Louis Salmon, who died at age 70 early Sunday morning at home?

Roscoe Roberts Jr. spent three-plus decades practicing law in a firm that was Watts, Salmon, Roberts, Manning and Noojin before it became Lange, Simpson, Robinson and Somerville.

In those 30-odd years, Roberts was able to observe, closely, his friend and business partner's total package: public demeanor, private life, hopes and dreams. So on a gorgeous fall Monday afternoon not suited for the somber duty of mourning, this was Roberts' response when asked who Louis Salmon really was:

"He was the nearest to a perfect human I've ever seen."

What helped Salmon be so successful at practicing law, sitting on many advisory boards and serving in numerous civic capacities all at the same time, said Roberts, was "his mind was so clear."

Armed with such a weapon while also possessing the inner drive of a man who never saw a problem he felt couldn't be solved, Salmon was, according to his friend and associate, "incomparable."

Incomparable: beyond comparison; unequaled; matchless.

What glowing tribute, even from a dear friend, yet Roberts said it's true and that Salmon's "retinue of allegiances" would substantiate it if they all came forward.

But since bombast and breast beating weren't his way, no one, not even close and true friends, knows exactly how many other close and true friends Salmon really had.

Roberts believes they are legion, just as he believes Salmon "had more virtues and less faults than any person I ever ran across."

In spite of always being busier than any five men, Salmon "always took time to stop and visit for a moment, and it wasn't just a pat-on-the-back kind of thing," said his friend.

The mind of Salmon, the weapon that helped set him apart from the herd, "was so well-organized he could accomplish more in an hour than most people could in two or three. His law partners could work 24 hours a day and not keep up with him. He could do more on the phone in an afternoon than I could do in isolation." Roberts also revealed this telling insight into his old friend: "Never, never would he be part of any questionable conduct. He simply didn't cut any corners. He wouldn't have anything to do with those who did."

Salmon was, Roberts said, "the most loyal person I've ever met. He was loyal to his friends and to his ideals. But he was no milquetoast. You always knew exactly where he stood."

He was "a wonderful family man, and when one of his children had problems, they were his problems."

Although he "did things without fanfare" and didn't "go looking for civic responsibilities," Salmon never shirked those duties, either, and because of that, "All those who make up Huntsville are the beneficiaries."

To furnish a complete answer to the question of who Louis Salmon was, Roberts also said this: "He had all the virtues I'd ever want in a son, and I loved him very much."

(September 28, 1993)

Just Being Different
Was Normal for Tillman

This is what he said in the introduction to "Mr. Anderson's Monument," the book he wrote about growing up as a mill village boy: "Have you ever noticed how easy it is to forget bad times, and the good times get better and better?"

It was more than just a question; it summarized his philosophy.

"Tillman Hill was free-hearted with everybody," said Betty Stewart Hill, who was 16 when she started dating him and was married to him for 47 years.

"I don't care if you knocked him or bumped him," said she, "he was never negative."

While others loved wallowing in the slop of self-pity, her husband chose to always travel the high road.

He wouldn't even take a detour when his enemies once tried to drag his good name through political mud.

After being accused of accepting land from a builder in exchange for doing road work in a subdivision, Betty said she was "real upset and wanted to do something bad to them." But her husband calmly said, "Betty, please don't think of them like that. Let's just put this behind us."

A jury proclaimed him not guilty by a vote of 11-to-1 and charges were dropped, but instead of trying to get even like most men would, he channeled his enormous energy into being the best he could be at what he was doing.

History will one day record that Tillman Hill was a great member of the Madison County Commission.

He didn't have college degrees but he did have a great deal of common sense, which is probably more important. He saw things from the perspective of working people, and made his decisions accordingly. It was familiar ground for him, for he had been "a working man" from about age 10.

He never was ashamed of being born in a mill village. In fact, he wore it on his chest like Superman wears his "S." When he reached maturity, lessons he learned as a hard-nosed youth helped him become a man among men.

He got his outrageous sense of humor from Hobart and Sallie Hill, the parents he worshiped, who also taught him fairness, loyalty, love and honor.

He was a barrel-chested Huntsville Times pressman and I was 19 and green when we met. He grinned and said he'd love to show me the ropes. It was a fruitful friendship which led to my helping him edit his 1996 book about living in

Lincoln village.

The cancer that killed him Tuesday was really working him over during the year we spent putting the book together, but I never saw him flinch.

He lasted as long as he did because his extraordinary heart wouldn't stop pumping an overpowering will to live through his veins.

Hobart and Sallie had also taught him not to be a quitter.

His refusal to die caused a nurse attending him in his last weeks of life to declare, "This just isn't normal."

But those who knew him best, like his son, Dee, his daughter, Diane, and his grandsons, Gary Alan and Todd, knew better.

(January 15, 1998)

The Keeper of the Door Is a Winner

"Accept what you have and do with it the best you can. Play the hand the Lord dealt you to the hilt. And bear in mind you're not going to be able to play it by yourself."

--Bill Whatley, Feb. 28, 1990

As you would expect, several airplane pictures hang on Huntsville Aviation General Manager William R. "Bill" Whatley's office walls. But plaques and citations given to him by Shrine and Crippled Children's hospitals and local group for the handicapped outnumber them. Airplane photos signify a successful business. Plaques and citations signify a successful life. You get the impression he's prouder of the latter.

Born in the small Dale County town of Skipperville 60 years ago, he knew from an early age he'd never be like his eight brothers and sisters. For he was born with spina bifida and his body won't work from the waist down. "But I was lucky," he said. "Some have no use of their limbs from the neck down."

He had his first operation at 5 and was "sent

home to die." When he didn't, other surgery followed. He hasn't kept count, but estimated he's been operated on more than 20 times.

He was also lucky enough to be born into the right family. His father, a saw mill worker and former cowboy, was a person "who got mad when it got dark and he couldn't work anymore. He instilled that work ethic in us. It's not being done much anymore."

His parents insisted he go to school when others said don't bother, he's going to die. His parents said, "He may die in school, but he's going to school." His brothers put him in a little red wagon and pulled him there. Later, he went to college and learned how to keep books.

Which is how he ended up running Huntsville Aviation. He answered an ad Montgomery Aviation placed in a newspaper for a bookkeeper. He was eventually elected secretary-treasurer of the company, allowed to buy some stock, and the owner, Bob Hudgens, sent him to open the Huntsville operation. "But what about," he asked Hudgens, "my physical condition?" Hudgens replied, "What physical condition?" It was exactly the attitude he had grown up with around his family. He came here in 1965 and learned management "by the seat of my pants."

To get around, Whatley uses a cane, crutches or his motorized wheelchair. One night, he said, going from his office across to the terminal at

Huntsville International Airport for an Airport Authority meeting, security guards clocked him on their radar gun at 7 mph in his chair. He's a member of civic clubs, freely gives his time to handicapped-oriented groups and is determined to make Huntsville Aviation "a front door to this community, because this is the first and last impression many businessmen have of Huntsville."

Married to the former Betty Word of Scottsboro for 14 years, Bill Whatley is a complex man in a simple way. He has never drawn unemployment because "Daddy taught me better." He has learned you can find humor in life if you look for it. And he said two of his greatest pleasures are working with young people and working with the handicapped.

Reportedly the oldest "active spina bifida patient in America," he said he supposes in his case, "It's your faith in the Lord, what you've got left inside, and what your ancestors put in you." And Bill Whatley said when the time comes, this is what he'd like to have written beside his name: "That I tried to impart to my fellow man what I learned from my fellow man."

(March 1, 1990)

He'd Rather Take
to the Bright Side

SCOTTSBORO -- Jephthah. A biblical name. Shortened so the Moody men are just called Jep.

Jep, Jep II, Jep III; grandfather, father, son.

Jep Moody II, president and chairman of the board of Jacobs Bank, aimed his automated wheelchair with the orange and blue Auburn bumper sticker toward some shade near the clubhouse of Goosepond Colony golf course and screeched to a halt.

"It's easy to drive this thing when you've had as much practice as me," he said, a happy smile wreathing his face.

Smiling wasn't always easy, until he figured out the alternative.

"I'm lucky to be alive," he said near the end of the bank's 22nd annual golf tournament Wednesday.

When diagnosed with Guillain-Barre syndrome in 1984, Mayo Clinic doctors said it was the worst case they'd seen for somebody to survive. Most people recover from the nerve disease. Jep was near death for months, spending 15 months in bed before beginning therapy which has him where he is today.

"People who haven't seen me in a long time say I'm doing better, but I think I've reached a plateau and I don't think I'll ever do better than this." It was said matter-of-fact, no complaints. "But I can use a walker a little," he added, his way of putting a positive light on his plight.

Jep Moody II and his friend Shorty Robertson loved golf so much they started the Jacobs Bank tournament to show their appreciation of the game and for their friends.

Mostly out-of-town bankers and some close Jacobs Bank Jackson County friends participated early on. But as popular as Shorty and Jep were, the tournament couldn't help growing. Wednesday, a picture-perfect day when Goosepond's geese were in full performance, 144 players teed off.

"It's 'bout got too big," said Jep, taking the name of another golfer who wants to play next year. "If it's not too big to handle, I want to keep on having it." He didn't say how big too big is.

Shorty Robertson died in December of 1984, just months after Jep's illness was diagnosed, and it seemed the triumphant twosome would become a memory.

Jep wouldn't have that. He was too something: stubborn, lucky. Now Shorty's still fondly remembered each time Jep hosts the tournament in the spring.

Wednesday, while sunshine glinted off the green golf course grass and flying geese honked a symphony, the bank president looked at the beauty of the day and said, "You know you do (get frustrated). But I don't feel sorry for myself. I'm thankful I can do what I do."

When he played, Jep scored in the high 70s and low 80s, and friends said nobody competed harder or loved the game more passionately than the Auburn engineering graduate who once studied Chinese at Yale University.

He'd still love to play. "You know I would," he said, smile broadening, brightening. "I'd love to get up out of this chair right here and take some swings."

Running the tournament has to satisfy his passion for the game now, but Jep Moody II accepts no pity and has no regrets.

"Sometimes it's hard going to the golf course to see the fellows going off to play," he said. "But I try to always think on the bright side. I'm just lucky to be here."

(March 1, 1990)

He's Keeping the Promise
and Smelling the Roses

"Old lawyers never die or retire. They just lose their appeal." Bill Galloway chuckled after sharing that bit of legal frivolity Thursday, the day before being pitched a going-away party by friends. After 38-plus years, being a lawyer "is not as much fun as it used to be," so at the ripe old age of not-yet-65, Galloway's taking down his shingle. He's keeping a promise he made to himself several years ago driving home from the funeral of a prominent Huntsville lawyer.

"I decided that day I wanted to stop and smell some roses before I start pushing them up at Maple Hill," he said. Things have changed dramatically during the lifetime of this native Huntsvillian. His parents told him he was the only baby in Huntsville Hospital on the day he was born (Aug. 30, 1932). "Now you can't stir them with a stick," he quipped.

There were only 50 or 60 lawyers in town when he began his career as the first associate of the firm of Ford, Caldwell, Ford and Payne in February 1959 after serving two years in the Army's Counterintelligence Corps, "but there are probably over 400 today."

In fact, Huntsville has so many lawyers, and the state's three law schools are graduating so many potential lawyers every year, Galloway fears a good many of them won't be able to earn a living.

Then there's the growing trend toward specialization, which means, he said, "learning more and more about less and less."

He became a specialist, too, in real estate law, and proclaimed himself "Dean of the Probate Record Room."

"It's not as dramatic as murder cases," he said, "but it puts meat and potatoes on the table."

He got into this particular field of law when Joe Payne, the firm's real estate specialist, was called back to active military service in 1962 during the Cold War when Soviet Premier Nikita Khrushchev made some threatening noises.

He switched to real estate law because Huntsville was having one of its growth spurts at the time Payne was recalled.

"I've always had a soft spot for Khrushchev because he changed my career," Galloway said.

He met Mary Ellen Masters in 1956 when they were freshmen at Vanderbilt. They got married and had three sons - Glenn, Andrew and Tom. None of them are lawyers, which suits their father, who said he saw his own future when he was just a lad of 12.

"I can still see Mr. Earl (Ford) walking on the square in his white Palm Beach suit in the hottest part of the year. They told me he was a lawyer. I knew I wanted to be one," Galloway said. He is happy with his decision. "I had a good practice and it was a good life," he said. "But now it's time to move on."

He knows he'll be busy in retirement because his wife has prepared "a long list of honey-dos." But for the first six months, "I'm gonna sit on my back porch in a rocking chair. Then after six months, I'm gonna start rocking."

(June 29, 1997)

Sitting Down to a Banquet
of Memories

"School exists for the population that inhabits it at the moment. It has to change. You have to let it grow."

-- Tom Owen, head football coach, high school principal, philosopher.

Today's the last day in the storied coaching and teaching career of Tom Owen, but like everything else he's ever done, he can't just walk away.

When Lee High School's faculty and staff begins the new school year Monday, each will get a letter from the man who for 11 years was their principal.

Typically Owen, the letter contains this paragraph: "Robert Louis Stevenson postulates that `sooner or later in life, everyone sits down to a banquet of memories.' As the shadows of my life grow taller you will be ever present in my banquet of memories. As Dag Hammersjold said, "for all that has been, thanks, for all that is to come, yes."'

You must remember he was first a history teacher, and they are expected to quote famous writers and general secretaries of the United

Nations.

That Owen shows concern for the faculty and staff that served him so well for more than a decade won't surprise those who know him. Especially those who played for him when he was head football coach at Huntsville High before lupus ended what had the makings of a legendary career. Because the man still called "Coach" 20 years after being forced from the sidelines has always stood up for his team.

He had one goal when he became history teacher and head football coach in his hometown of Webster, Fla., in 1954 as a 22-year-old fresh out of Florida State University.

"I thought if I could ever get to be head coach at Daytona Beach Mainland, I'd stay there the rest of my life." Mainland was one of the top three prep jobs in Florida then. He got it early in the 1960s and felt he was set, until Huntsville High changed the course of his life in 1964 by making an offer he couldn't refuse.

Mary Frances Joiner was a FSU majorette plus a member of the school circus, Tarpon Swim Club and Gymkana team. She was also the only woman Tom Owen wanted, so they married while still attending FSU. Mary taught for 30 years at Jones Valley school before retiring in June. They have two sons, Tommy, 37, and Tighe, 33.

Owen was a fine coach (145 wins, 75 losses) who turned out to be a fine principal who is as proud of his "big wins" in administration as he is of those in football.

He feels modern culture has taught young people that "if you hit them they hit back, if you shout at them they shout back. If you have a fight and lose, we used to get embarrassed, but now they get a gun. We've got to find some way to stop that."

Yet he believes "the overwhelming majority of students want to do the right thing and work hard," despite "disturbing trends" involving those who make trouble in school.

If he hadn't had lupus, Tom Owen might have built one of the South's great high school coaching records or landed a college coaching job. He has no regrets and is not disappointed. "It was," he said, "time for me to change, and I have enjoyed being an administrator immensely."

In retirement, he plans to do consulting, play lots of golf "and spend the rest of my life paying Mary back, because all of this was made possible by her allowing me the latitude."

(August 12, 1994)

Kids Were Special to Candy Man

Even though the message was simple, it spoke volumes. "We Will Miss You Candy Man," said the words on the ribbon on the wreath. Candy Man would have smiled if he could have read it.

Thomas H. "Tooney" Summers was interested in many things. From politics to sports, if he liked it, it got his full attention. And children, his or yours, never failed to receive a full dose of tender loving care.

At Weatherly Heights Church of Christ, his coat pockets filled with candy, Tooney stood by the door before and after services to give the youngest children pieces of candy.

It became a ritual, little kids tugging at his coat and asking, "What do you have for us today?"

Sometimes if older children, those 10 or 12, stopped to watch the young ones get their treats, Tooney motioned to them and said, "Come here and I'll give you a piece, too."

Tooney wasn't bent on spoiling children, he just wanted them to have more than he did as a kid.

Two floral arrangements at his funeral Sunday would have been real special to him. One was a big wreath with candy on it, the other was a basket of flowers with candy in it. They were from the children of the church, and included the ribbon about missing him.

Lots of people will miss Tooney Summers, as evidenced by a standing-room-only gathering which came to Weatherly Heights to say farewell to a man who meant much to Huntsville and Madison County.

His friends included politicians of the highest rank, famous sports personalities and successful men and women from the business world.

That list also included those not so fortunate, but the beauty of Tooney was you didn't have to be high and mighty to earn his friendship. In fact, it's possible he felt kinder and closer toward have-nots than toward haves.

Tooney must have been a happy, contented man, because I never saw him without a smile on his face. It was an original, genuine smile that belonged only to him. And if you ever made the mistake of asking about his family, the smile broadened and soon stretched from ear-to-ear.

Although he talked intricate politics or practical baseball with equal expertise, he wasn't at all a complex man. What you saw was what you got. And even if he wasn't perfect, you knew you could depend on what he said.

Tooney made some money, but you'd never know it from the way he acted. A good portion of the money he made also showed up in other pockets, because he was one of those who positively would rather give than receive. Handing out candy to children was just one of the good traits he demonstrated.

Maybe he was happy and unselfish because verse one of Psalm 46 was one of his favorite Bible passages: "God is our refuge and strength, a very present help in trouble."

Alabama Head Coach Gene Stallings was one of those who attended the funeral. Auburn Assistant Coach Wayne Hall was a pallbearer. Through the sadness and the tears, their presence moved one of Tooney's sons to note, "Daddy would have died for this."

Tooney Summers would have loved that one, and if the Candy Man did hear it, I guarantee there was a big smile on his face.

(May 4, 1993)

Curtain Call for the Girl
on the News

She changed from young girl to grown woman before our eyes, a delightful experience for those who watched the metamorphosis. We invited her into our homes twice a night for over 15 years because she was comfortable, believable and the girl next door all in one.

In a business encouraging glitz and glitter, she never lost sight of what her role was or what she wanted to be: a very good reporter. Now the curtain falls tonight on a Tennessee Valley institution.

The 10 o'clock news on Channel 48 will be Missy Ming's last telecast. Missy Ming Smith, wife of Judge Lynwood Smith for the last three years, first female evening news anchor in Alabama, leaves the stage with bittersweet memories but no regrets as to the quality of her contributions.

Fresh out of Auburn in 1975, Channel 19 hired her as a reporter. The next fall, General Manager Tom Purcer offered her a co-anchor spot with Tom Kennemer. The two have been a team ever since, first at 19, then at 48, where they moved in 1981. She recalled 19 raised her from minimum wage to

$100 a week when she joined Kennemer on the anchor desk.

She said this of her longtime partner: "Tom Kennemer is a good man. He's just an old country boy from Brindlee Mountain. He's always been very supportive of me, and I of him, and that's why we stayed together. But when she pioneered the female as evening news anchor in Alabama, "I didn't want to choose between anchor and reporter." Nor did she want to be "just an ornament."

So she anchored both evening newscasts and did pieces of reporting. It created 14-hour days. Single, when she got home she told Buffy, her Cocker Spaniel who's now 16, all about her day.

Enter The Judge. Rather, she entered his office one day to ask about a child custody case. Judge Smith said she didn't ask, but "stood there with hands on hips and demanded." They went out to dinner. They hit it off. They got married. Missy Ming came to Huntsville with her parents, Art and Attie. He was with the Pershing Missile Project. She attended Whitesburg School through third grade, then graduated from Athens High after her parents bought a farm in Limestone County.

At Auburn, she was going to study microbiology, "It didn't fit my personality." So she switched to the School of Communications and landed the Channel 19 job on her first stab. In her 15-plus years in television, her favorite stories were "the small ones: farmers and their crops, a family raising tobacco in Lincoln County, interviews with children."

She's proud "my position had substance to it, that I was a working journalist, that I never compromised my ethics, and that I never lied." She's "excited" about her new job as director of information and community relations for Madison County.

"It was very, very hard when management informed me I was leaving." she said. "But God doesn't close one door without opening another. Now I'll still be able to give to people and the community like I always have."

On this sad, final day, Missy Ming Smith's thoughts will be on the "many, many wonderful viewers who watched me over the years.

"But I walk away with a good feeling."

(January 17,1991)

In Praise of an Elegant Lady's Life

BIRMINGHAM -- One of my favorite memories happened one night when two of the state's famous sportsmen engaged in playful give-and-take.

It was at an Alabama Sports Hall of Fame dinner where Fred Sington Sr., former Alabama Crimson Tider from Birmingham, and Frank Howard, former Clemson football coach who was born in Barlow Bend, entertained with tales of those bygone days when they were teammates in Tuscaloosa.

Coach Howard, who once was one of the most-demanded after-dinner speakers in America, was comfortable with a microphone in his hand, and therefore rambled on-and-on about how it was to be in college with "Football Freddy" Sington. When he finally got his chance, Mr. Sington laid into his old buddy with both fists, verbally speaking, and soon had the hall rocking with laughter.

But just when it seemed he had built up a good head of steam, the woman seated beside him started tugging at his coattail. Football Freddy abruptly stopped the story he was telling. "She's saying for me to sit down," he said.

And he did.

It couldn't have been easy being the wife of one of the state's leading citizens and the matriarch of one of the University of Alabama's first families, but Nancy Napier Sington proved to be more than equal to the task.

She was 22 when she married Fred Sington, who was 24. He was an All-American football player at Alabama, a Rose Bowl star, the subject of the song "Football Freddy" written by Rudy Vallee, and had set out to make his mark as a major league baseball player.

This was in The Great Depression, but Nancy stood solidly beside Fred in his attempt to become a big leaguer. Years later, she was still his best friend when he opened what became the state's preferred chain of sporting goods stores. And always, she was there for their sons, Fred Jr., David and Leonard.

Yet her world didn't completely revolve around what her men did. She always had a mind of her own and a personal agenda steeped in service. Organizations like Daughters of the American Revolution and the Salvation Army had in her a champion forever ready to fight for their causes.

Although she lived life and pursued dreams in a quiet, dignified way, she could often be too honest and outspoken for her own good. "Straightforward, to a fault," is how her pastor, Dr. Scott McClure, described her. But her friendly

103

manner and pleasing personality made her a multitude of friends of all ages, most of whom came Friday to tell her goodbye.

In a 30-minute service as elegant as she was, Nancy Napier Sington was eulogized for being a true and faithful wife and companion to the husband she loved for 60 years. She was celebrated for being mother to three male children who each have some of her strong, distinctive personality. She was remembered as a friend of all mankind, rich, poor or indifferent.

She was a warm and friendly lady who liked to give hugs and be hugged, and those who knew her will be a long time getting over the fact she's gone. Yet her life will continue to live in the lives of her children and their children.

Most assuredly, she will live in the memory of Fred Sington Sr., the man she shared her life with for so many years and the man who was with her when her life quietly ended.

(July 24, 1994)

IV. Making a Difference

He Made His Special Gift Take Flight

Donald Dupree didn't brag about being a medical marvel. He was too thankful to waste the few extra years he got by being big-headed. After all, he knew better than most that time is precious, that his was limited, that he'd be foolish to squander it.

He took part in medical history Christmas Eve, 1987, by becoming one of only 15 people to have received a "piggy-back" heart transplant where a donor heart is attached to the original.

When he died late last week, he and only one other person had survived the process. His condition made him the subject of stories in newspapers and medical journals, all of which dealt mostly with scientific data and not the man.

In 1976, Donald and Barbara Dupree built a home on what once was the Dupree family farm's livestock pasture in the Monrovia community. The house included a room for Barbara's mother, Ora Gentle Bristor. She and Donald became best friends, and in the years after his transplant the woman called "Big Momma" looked after him like he was her son.

This affection was a bonus for a man whose sister, nieces and female cousins already loved him to pieces. A bonus because he had both his wife and his mother.

Zuba McDonald Dupree lives across the road from Mt. Zion Baptist Church on the spot where she lived when her children, Gerald, Donald and Janice, were born. Three Dupree brothers lived side-by-side on that road, and though this big country family eventually scattered, Zuba stayed where it all began. Her son Donald built his home in the field behind her.

After two stillborn babies, Barbara and Donald adopted Jason when he was 4 months old. Now he's 15. His father's transplant gave them six more years together, crucial years in the life of an adolescent boy.

With an extra chance, Donald devoted himself to being husband, father, brother and friend. He continued pursuing his love of law enforcement with the Huntsville Police Department, too. But most of all, he dedicated himself to assisting people.

Money he helped raise for Huntsville Hospital Foundation heart research numbers in the thousands of dollars. Hours he gave to the Alabama Organ Center and the UAH Hospital

Heart-Lung Transplant Support Group are countless. Transplant patients he helped came to his visitation Sunday night and to his funeral Monday.

Barbara Dupree said her husband had quietly started putting his house in order. He bought her a new car "because he wanted me to have a good one." He made sure details concerning her and Jason were taken care of. He bought the suit, tie and shirt he was buried in.

Just as someone had donated him a heart, he also showed the kind of man he had become by donating his eyes. Barbara said the family of the young man whose heart her husband got "gave us a gift, and Donald worked very hard to protect that gift. He exercised and he did the right things. I hope whoever got his eyes appreciates them as much as he did that heart."

Donald Dupree chose to stay close to his roots. They buried him behind the church across the road from the place where he was born, and only a little ways from where he stayed to live.

But though he didn't roam too far from his small community, his influence was felt in faraway places. And because a young man gave him a few extra years of precious life, he was able to give someone else the wonderful gift of sight.

(March 29, 1994)

It Was an Honor to Be Her Friend

The first thing I had to do after being hired at *The Huntsville Times* was go to the business office and fill out necessary forms. "Find Opal and she'll take good care of you," said Will Mickle, the paper's editor. "Be nice," he cautioned. "She signs the paychecks every week."

It was 1959, I was 19 years old, and, although I didn't know it, about to meet a woman I would fall in love with. In the years they worked together at *The Times*, Opal Dilworth, Virginia Bowers Upton and Frances Richards were as close a threesome as ever was put together. If you saw one chances are the other two weren't far away. Jack Langhorne, the publisher and possessor of a laid-back sense of humor, fondly called them "The Gold Dust Twins" even though they were a trio.

They were given another nickname when Leroy Simms became publisher of *The Times*. They were called "Leroy's Angels" after "Charlie's Angels," the television show which featured three ladies bringing gangsters and other no-goods to justice. If Opal, Virginia and Frances weren't quite the visible and avenging angels as Charlie's were, they nonetheless served important roles for their boss,

Leroy.

Before marrying Jack Dilworth, Opal was a member of the New Hope branch of the Hornbuckle family. It was, and is, a large family. Her parents had 11 children alone, and she loved telling me and anyone else who'd listen about her brothers and sisters.

What I remember most, though, is how Opal ("Don't call me Mrs. Dilworth") took an almost-maternal interest in me and my career. Maybe it was because she didn't have a son, I don't know. But during the 26 years we worked in the same building before she retired in 1985, many were the times she stopped me in the hall to compliment something I'd written or to tell me she heard So-and-So spreading rumors about my conduct.

If she had ever asked me if the rumors were true, I'd have told her the truth. I know she didn't always approve of the attitude I projected in those days, but she encouraged me to be a good person more times than she scolded me for being a bad one. Being a fine, Christian person herself, there's no doubt in my head now that she knew better than I did what was best for me.

One thing I'm thankful for is she lived long enough to see me change my wicked ways, and I know that meant something to her because she loved me. I know that because one of her nieces reinforced it Tuesday. Marcie Brown looked me square in the face at the cemetery and said, "She loved you."

This was after a lovely funeral service had sent Opal Hornbuckle Dilworth on her way to heaven, a service in which we all celebrated her joyful life with some lighthearted anecdotes. At the funeral home Monday night, Opal lay in state in a pink dress with her favorite pearl necklace. I always thought she was pretty in pink. At the head of her casket was a bouquet of yellow roses, her favorite flowers, sent by her best buddies, Frances and Virginia.

I heard a lady who knew Opal from either the Pilot Club, the Lifeline volunteer group, the Kiwanis Auxiliary or the First United Methodist Church tell some others at the visitation, "It was an honor to be her friend."

It sure was. And when Will Mickle hired me all those years ago he didn't know what a prophet he would be when he told me if I would go and find Opal she'd take good care of me.

(February 9, 1994)

He Was of a Special Generation

Joyful is the best way to describe being in the company of quiet, selfless dignity which shines like a lighthouse on a perilous coast. J.B. Burkett worked hard all his life, but rather than complain, he celebrated the fact his hands were calloused and his back was sore. Although he lived a simple life, he wasn't a simple man. Yet you wouldn't classify him as complex, either. Calling him a paradox is closer to the truth, for he lived his plain and simple life with the native intelligence and common sense so characteristic of his generation.

He was the father of my best friend's wife, and when they buried him Monday it felt like a member of my family had died, too. If it's true God works in mysterious ways, He and J.B. did it up right this time. Only a few months shy of his 85th birthday, Mr. Burkett was killed in a car wreck only about a mile from his home. He probably shouldn't have been driving, but stubbornness was one of his traits, too.

It took stubborn people working in Southern textile mills, Northern steel mills, Western fruit fields and Midwestern wheat fields to survive the Great Depression, and J.B. Burkett was most

111

certainly a true son of his generation. He would tell you about the hard times if you asked, but when he told it he included the fact he thanked God just for the opportunity of giving him a chance to survive. When he was called home to glory on that bridge crossing the Flint River near Walnut Grove, J.B. had been married to Bessie Burkett for more than 60 years, which is another clue he was from a generation of Americans we're not used to reading about today. To return to his roots, he moved from town to the country several years ago and was able to spend the remainder of his life in the kind of atmosphere that made him happy.

He loved his place on Upcreek Road with the river flowing near and nature all around. In fact, the blanket on his casket was weaved from his favorite bushes and trees. There would have been another of those quick, easy smiles on his crinkled, friendly face if he could have seen it. They said he said all the squirrels around his house knew his name, and who's to say they didn't, for his was a loving, gentle nature whose spirit radiated trust. Late on an afternoon when shadows were long and dusk was gathering, it's easy to imagine him talking quietly to the squirrels and birds as he fed them. The roll call of men cut from the same cloth J.B. Burkett was cut from grows shorter, for he, like his peers, was truly a Renaissance Man, one capable of figuring out in his head how a thing had to be done and then using his hands to do it. For him, that was part of the joy of simply being alive. For him, that was the sum total of truthful existence. Now his life is over, but it won't be forgotten, for it will remain in a special place in the hearts of his wife and children, and it will always live on the faces of his grandchildren.

(April 25, 1995)

His Picture Should Be
By the Word "Courage"

Webster's New World Dictionary defines courage as an attitude of facing and dealing with anything recognized as dangerous, difficult or painful instead of withdrawing from it. The dictionary people must have had in mind the man I'm writing about today when they penned their definition.

His name was Charles Grayson, but everybody called him "Chuck." Already an advertising salesman for The Huntsville Times when I began my career, Chuck became one of those I felt comfortable around. His personality was friendly and outgoing, plus he was from my side of town. Anyone who grew up eating biscuits at Aunt Eunice's, dipped dogs at Zesto's and hamburgers at Mullins' can't be all bad.

Chuck didn't come to work one day. He'd had a bad stroke, we were told. If he lived, everyone was pretty sure, he would never be able to work again. Well, not only did he live, he came back to selling ads, and this is where the part about courage begins.

A debilitating stroke is one of the worst indignities a human has to endure. If it was painful for his friends to watch Chuck trying to overcome it, imagine how painful it must have been for him. Yet there he was, taking his medicine and his painful therapy every day and doing his job, too, trying with all of his big heart to get better, to be as good as he once had been.

Chuck was a relatively young man when this happened, but what I remember most is he didn't want us to pity him, he wanted us to support him. We supported him, but we also admired him, for he seemed to symbolize how a man with spirit can dodge the potholes on the surface of life's highway.

Our paper has an employee golf tournament every year, and none of us could believe it when Chuck said he was playing in it the first spring after his stroke. He lasted all 18 holes, and those of us playing behind him could barely see our own golf balls through the tears in our eyes. That wonderful lesson in courage we learned that day is the first thing I thought about this week when I heard Chuck had died. He suffered so much in the last two years, his indomitable spirit finally had to yield.

He told Betty, his wife, "I want you to quit pushing me, I'm tired," and she said, "Baby, I know you are." His long struggle ended with a peaceful death in his sleep.

Saturday morning, Betty Grayson took a break

from answering the cards of sympathy she has received to say her husband had fought "so long and so hard" that the conflict finally wore him out.

"He was ready to go," she said, "and I'm not worried about where he is today." She said the only real thing bothering her now is that their grandchildren, one age 9 and the other 4, "will have to grow up not knowing what a wonderful grandfather they had."

Then Betty Grayson said she hopes if their children learned anything from Chuck Grayson, it was this: "You just don't give up. You just keep on trucking."

(October 26, 1997)

A Voyage of Enrichment Continues

HARVEST -- So much has happened in Hattie McFarlen Freeman's lifetime, it's hard to say what's impressed her most. But she's sure "a computer is the strangest thing" ever invented in her 96 years on Earth.

Hattie McFarlen was born in 1898 "up Clear Creek" in Jackson County. She attended a one room school made of logs where literature and history were her best subjects. There the idea of going to the Old North Church in Boston "was planted in my mind." Many years later, she and her husband, Earl Freeman, flew to Massachusetts to see where Paul Revere began his midnight ride.

With a sweet smile on her friendly face, Hattie says it was her "greatest thrill" and is "sorry I couldn't have lived way back yonder" since the idea of pioneers and pioneering has stuck with her all the way from Clear Creek to Harvest Road.

Harvest Road was gravel 62 years ago when she and Earl, now 89, moved into their little three-room house with its green tin top. They had been married three years, starting late in matrimony, Hattie said, "because one old man did me dirty." Earl Freeman won her hand "because I thought he was honest and could be respected."

Years passed and two children, Nancy (Hughes) and Jimmy, were born. They added to the house, which became a three-bedroom home with indoor plumbing. Now the children are gone and there are six grandchildren and three great-grandchildren, "but unless we win one of those sweepstakes," the Freemans plan to stay where they are.

The yearning to learn has never left Hattie Freeman, who got her General Education Development (GED) high school diploma when she was 78. Earl drove her 30 miles roundtrip daily to Ardmore so she could attend classes "just to learn. I knew at that age I was too old to work."

She would have gone to college to learn more, but couldn't drive. Now at 96, and although "there's nothing wrong with my mind, it's my body that's giving out," she believes she could still be driving if she had learned how. Even though she loves to grow flowers (roses are her favorite), Hattie says "people are my hobby." She hosts several Christmas parties each year for people in the Harvest community. This year's plans include a catered dinner for 30 couples at a local church's activity center, just for the socializing.

The idea came from George and Dottie Epps, who started inviting people from the community to their Independence Day family barbecue about 20 years ago.

"I reckon I think I'm gonna live forever," Hattie

said. "I plan things for the future. But I've got the best health of anybody around." Although long life runs in the family tree of Hattie McFarlen Freeman, she has a decided opinion about the source of her longevity:

"Don't forget, I learned about God wandering on those mountains in Jackson County. I'd see all those flowers and things. That's been my mainstay, and I think that's why I've lived so long."

(November 8, 1994)

Like Two Sparrows in a Hurricane

LAGRANGE, Ga. -- If it was hard being married to a high-profile preacher whose life never really has been his own, she didn't show it. For the record, her husband has always said without her he couldn't have shouldered the cross God told him to bear.

From the moment they became partners almost 51 years ago, she handled the pressure of being his wife with a grace and a dignity which grew to be legendary. If he was the hurricane, then she was the eye of the storm, and her tranquil soul and sweet spirit provided safe harbor where he could rest and refresh, knowing full well she would fit together the bits and pieces of family life without him directly being involved except when needed.

He could concentrate on preaching with crystal clear clarity the uncompromised word of God. He could conduct the Lord's business every day without interference. She was his mighty fortress, and the ministry of Jesus Christ prospered and grew because her presence allowed him to heed the call he received as a young man. It didn't hurt that she was as beautiful outside as she was inside, because the complete package encouraged and influenced many women, married and single, in churches where they served to improve themselves, spiritually as well as physically.

Vonzeal Davis Dorriety was no saint, but she was the closest to being one I've ever met. In a society that loves to use cliches just for the sound of them, she was a bonafide role model, the Real McCoy, a woman anybody would love to have as a wife, a mother, or a friend. Only Dr. James O. Dorriety could call her wife. Only Jerry and James Jr. could call her mother. But only God knows how many people got to call her friend.

Vonzeal Dorriety died Saturday, two months after being told she had six to eight weeks to live. Monday, Dr. Hugh Chambliss of Huntsville eulogized her and Dr. Charles Q. Carter of Atlanta preached her funeral. The old First Baptist Church in downtown LaGrange rang with Christian celebration for an hour, and most of the tears that rolled down cheeks and fell to the floor were tears of joy.

Eight weeks ago, when doctors gave the Dorriety family the sad news, she called her husband and her sons to her bedside and said: "We have told people all our lives how to live in the presence of God, and now we're going to show them how to do it."

She never complained and didn't cry during her painful ordeal. Even at the end of her life, she

121

handled the situation with her customary quiet, radiant grace. And she was, again, in the position of being a positive role model.

Terri Dorriety, 24, and a college student, said this: "My grandmother taught me how to comb my hair and how to coordinate my clothes. She taught me how to live life like a lady. Now she has taught me how to die with dignity."

Vonzeal Davis was 15 and they "waited" until Jim Dorriety was 18 before marrying in 1942. Monday, he said they'd found themselves another favorite love song in the last few weeks, a current country hit called "Like Two Sparrows in a Hurricane." His favorite part goes like this:

"She had his ring on her finger and he had the key to her heart."

(May 25, 1993)

On a Day When News Brought Tears

Things seemed normal at Parkway Lanes mid-afternoon Wednesday. A bowler practiced in solitude on one lane. Another man concentrated on a pinball machine. But sad silence covered the scene that even balls thrown by the lone bowler couldn't break. A couple of hours earlier, the bad news everybody expected, but dreaded, arrived. Pie was gone. Pam, who runs the lounge, cried openly. Behind the front counter, Joann's eyes were red-rimmed as she tried hard to stay composed. And Momma Jones, the cook, came out of the kitchen with tears rolling down her cheeks. "I loved him like a son," Momma sobbed, "and he loved me."

Roy "Pie" Bates, World War II medal winner, benefactor of many who needed a stake and champion of the handicapped, died Wednesday at age 65. He suffered for several weeks. They said his wife Sparky said he rested peacefully in the last half-hour of his life. He'll be remembered as a short man with a tall outlook. When he bought Parkway Lanes from Don Spencer in 1970, their contract was a handshake. Spencer knew that was enough. In later years, Pie sealed deals with others he helped with handshakes, too. It was his way. He was honest, so everybody else must be.

Roy Bates grew up poor in west Huntsville, but memories of his simple background weren't hard enough to erase the smile he always wore. One of his last pleasures was the fact protege Jimmy Certain was the Professional Bowling Association's senior bowler of the year in 1989. They were like father and son. It was Pie who advised, pampered and loved Jimmy in his down years, and it was Pie who helped sponsor him on the senior tour. On the night last January when Jim Certain was inducted into the Huntsville-Madison County Sports Hall of Fame, he fought back tears as he asked the crowd to help him remember his "little buddy" in their prayers.

But Pie's greatest joy was sponsoring the Parents of Exceptional People (PEP) bowling league.

It is a league for handicapped people 16 and over. Bates offered his bowling house, bought T-shirts and trophies, and sponsored the annual banquet.

Bowlers in that league call themselves the "Apple Pie Gang."

In 1983, Pie Bates said this when I asked him why he got involved in PEP:

"You go and watch them and it'll steal your heart. You sit there with a gloomy face and in comes a kid with a smile on his face who can't walk or talk. Yeah, I just did it because they became part of my life."

Wednesday, Joann bit her lip and said, "Pie was a good man. He and Sparky celebrated their 44th wedding anniversary in the hospital. And at least 50 people came."

The man who stood alone and played the pinball machine after the news of Pie's death reached Parkway Lanes was Herman Daniel, whose mother died only a few weeks ago.

Herman, Pie and three or four others played golf together for about 20 years, friends who shared each others' joys and heartaches.

The pinball game was Herman's way to escape, for a few minutes, the reality of what he'd been told.

"When I was bad sick for awhile," he said, "Pie never left me. He stayed with me all the way."

Now Roy "Pie" Bates will stay in the hearts and minds of all those who loved him.

(March 8, 1990)

Her Name's Just Simply Momma Jones

Momma Jones likes to come down some mornings and watch the women bowl. Old habits are hard to break. Until last fall, she spent 28 years of her life working at Parkway Lanes.

That's where she got the name "Momma." Parkway's late owner, Roy "Pie" Bates, started calling here that. After awhile, "Hardly anybody down here knew my real name," she said.

For the record, it's Mamie Lucille Gurley Davis Jones. Robert Adcock, who owned the bowling alley before Bates, called her "Flaming Mamie." But for year upon year, Parkway customers knew her simply as Momma Jones.

She was that sweet old lady with the quick smile and bountiful hugs who cooked in the kitchen. Cooked at several places before she came to Parkway in 1963. Cooked all of her life. Would still be cooking if Pie Bates hadn't died last March.

But after his death, new ownership decided to modernize the place, and because she missed Pie something fierce, Momma decided it was time to hang her apron up. "I just got to feeling I worked long enough," she said. Besides, she added, "I couldn't keep up with that old modern register because I'm still old-fashioned."

Momma Jones turned 80 last week. "But," said she, "I can't hardly realize I'm that old. I don't feel I'm 80. And I still praise God and thank Him for getting me up every morning and going about my business."

Would she like that business to include cooking burgers and fries for her regulars? "Oh, Lord yes!" she replied. "I get so bored sometimes I just get out and walk around the yard."

Mamie Lucille Gurley was born "somewhere near Triana." She finished the seventh grade at West Huntsville Middle School. "Daddy put us to work on the farm and we lived so far out in the country we didn't have a way to get to school," she said.

Her background, especially her mother's influence, instilled a tough independence. "I just don't like to be trouble to nobody, and I got that from my mother," she said. "My momma's been dead a long time, but every day she gets closer to me."

She has four children, two girls, two boys, from her marriage to W.E. Davis. Then she married Odie Jones. Both men are dead, but in addition to her children she has seven grandchildren, a step-granddaughter and two great-grandchildren.

While some women chattered and bowling balls

rumbled Wednesday morning, Momma Jones looked around Parkway Lanes and was overcome by memories.

"I still miss Pie," she said. "He was good to me, and he was too good for his own good. Those handicapped kids won his heart, and he thought they was it."

Those handicapped kids was a league for the retarded, sponsored by Bates.

"I loved Pie and I believe he loved me." She dabbed her eyes. "I had some good times down here."

At 80, eternity often enters Momma's mind now. "I feel God's presence all the time, and sometimes I just stop and start praying in the middle of the day. I believe when I get ready to leave this world, He's got my mansion ready for me."

Meanwhile, she's quietly comforted by faith and memories.

"I've had a good life," she said, with her trademark Momma Jones smile.

(February 28, 1991)

V. Blood Runs Thick

In the End, the Old Man
Is Forgiven by His Sons

The old man's sons spoke favorably of him at the memorial service last week, proving again that blood is often thicker than banishment. Banishment was self-imposed, for when he and the mother of their three children divorced, Sy Rathy took to the road.

He was one of the last of a breed -- an old-time salesman who went from town to town with his merchandise. In the last years of his career, he worked Alabama for Bulova Watch Co. Many jewelers he called on came to his funeral to pay their last respects. He was 81 when he just got tired and quit breathing in the wee hours of Saturday morning two weeks ago.

Although he hadn't smoked in 30 years, a touch of emphysema and some other pulmonary diseases weakened his already-weak condition. He had surgery for stomach cancer in August, seemed to have improved, but suffered a setback in late September from which he couldn't recover.

Sy lived by himself in a suite at the Executive Lodge for the last 10 years of his life, but he wasn't actually alone.

Many of the lodge's staff and other residents befriended the man they called "good," "kind" and "witty," and a note on the obituary provided by Laughlin Service Funeral Home said his survivors included "friends at the Executive Lodge."

One of those friends was Executive Lodge employee Kathy McClure, who in the seven years she knew Sy became like the daughter who wouldn't have anything to do with him.

Mrs. McClure knows his story well:

The son of Hungarian immigrants, Sy Rathy was born in New York in 1916. He had two sons and a daughter by his first wife. When his ex-wife decided to marry again, Sy wanted his children to be adopted by their stepfather "so their lives would be easier."

Then he went on the road, at one point having no contact at all with his children for 16 years because he felt they wanted to have nothing to do with him.

Then one of the sons had a baby daughter and sent her picture to the last address he had for his father. The picture made its way to Sy. Kathy McClure said Sy looked at the photograph and "cried like a baby" for an hour.

Contact was reunited with the sons. The daughter wouldn't budge. And for the rest of his life, Sy "worshiped his grandchildren from afar."

Once when a dentist suggested he pull and replace Sy's bad teeth, the old man said, "Why bother? How many more years do I have to use them? Besides, that would be taking money away from my kids."

When cancer was diagnosed, it was the sons who persuaded him to have surgery when their father at first stubbornly refused. And it was the sons who stood in the funeral home chapel to eulogize the father they hardly knew until both of them were grown.

Former Executive Lodge resident Connie Jones said Sy was "a very sweet man who could put a smile on your face."

Kathy McClure said it will take "a long, long time to get used to him not being here."

(October 14, 1997)

Happiness Is the Name
of the Game

SKINEM, Tenn. -- "Call me Bobbie 'cause my name's so stupid," Vonceil Smith Lindsey said, a rueful smile on her lips.

"Vonceil," she said slowly. "I think my daddy got it in France in World War I. I think he had a girlfriend with that name, only hers was spelled Von Ceil." Her nieces simply called her Bobbie when they couldn't pronounce Vonceil and it stuck. B&D Flea Market sits near Fayetteville in a curve on Old Huntsville Highway just over a rise from Albright's Grocery, which is at the intersection of County Road 110 in what Dee Lindsey calls "downtown Skinem."

"The flea market," he tried to say straight-faced, "is in north Skinem." Before it was a flea market, the place where Bobbie and Dee work and live was Tucker's Grocery. Mrs. Mattie Lou Tucker owned and ran it for 42 years, the last four with help from the Lindseys. She willed them the store when she died.

Before Mrs. Tucker, it was a honky tonk called the "Dipsey Doodle," then the "Evening Star" until the woman who owned it was murdered. Now the

Lindseys offer an assortment of collectibles there, including a sugar bowl 150 years old and some other objects from the last century. They even have a handwritten bill of sale for a 17-year-old female slave who sold for $550 in 1843. It's not for sale.

"How can we be married 51 years when I'm only about 56?" Dee protested when Vonceil mentioned their most recent anniversary.

She lived in Skinem and he lived in Lick Skillet in Madison County when they met at a party. Dee sang in a band, "and you know how you notice those guys playing music or in a uniform," Vonceil said. In fact, they both play musical instruments and sing, and obliged two visitors with a few numbers on the spot. They sang pure country without the condiments, squeezing every sweet sound available out of the well-used DoBro guitars they picked.

Vonceil's house had no electricity and the family used an outhouse when she married Dee in 1943. They were both 17 and he was about to spend two years in the Army in World War II. After the war, he went to work for Spur Oil Co. and stayed there until retiring in 1984. They came home to Skinem, then to the store a short distance down the road from where Vonceil lived as a girl.

They had four children, Royce, Danny and Rickey Lindsey, and Brenda Lindsey Minor, and they have five grandchildren and eight great-grandchildren. Royce died of cancer in 1992. Bobbie keeps a picture of him and her other three children on a counter in the store.

"It's been a good life," Dee said, stealing a glance at his wife. "I'd marry the same girl again." Outside the store, where tables and antiques are displayed to catch a traveler's eye, Dee Lindsey looked up and down the highway and pronounced Skinem to be "a good place to live. You don't make a lot of money. But if a man and his wife has got happiness, that's the name of the game."

(September 8, 1994)

Who'll Put the Pieces Together?

Glenda Faye Craig was all dressed up for her visitors Thursday. She wore a stunning pink dress with a white scarf. Her favorite locket hung from her neck. But Glenda couldn't hear how pretty everybody said she looked, couldn't respond to the terms of endearment whispered by her husband and parents, couldn't kiss the tears from her daughter's eyes. That's because she died Tuesday night, an innocent victim whose life was ended about 8 p.m. by a reckless, terrible act. She was only 25.

Glenda Craig was executed. That's the words her friends used. She happened to be the one behind the cash register when death came to the store where she worked. A man needed money. He robbed the place. Then shot Glenda in the head before leaving. It's all on video tape. The store had a surveillance camera. A suspect was arrested Wednesday morning.

And now the senseless shooting of Glenda Craig has utterly shattered and altered forever the lives of several people. The grieving parents will take her body home to North Carolina for burial, where they'll have to live with only memories of their vibrant, outgoing daughter.

Karen and Karla, the little girls, will no longer be in the comforting and warm embrace of their loving stepfather, for their father in North Carolina has decided they should live with him. And Darryl Craig has lost most of all. No more will have Glenda's love and friendship. No longer will he have the two black-eyed, dark-haired girls he treated as if they were his own. The person whose finger pulled the trigger that fired the gun that shot the bullet destroyed it all, and the broken pieces may never be put together again.

Glenda's husband and parents were too torn apart to talk about her at the funeral home. But they said friends and other family members could. And the story is this. The day his wife died was Darryl's first day back on his City-of Huntsville job after a lengthy absence because of a knee injury suffering playing basketball.

Since the injury wasn't job-related, there was no work compensation. Darryl's doctor advised him not to go back to work until November, but money got awfully short and he had no other choice. That's why Glenda was in the store to begin with. To "try to make ends meet," she worked about 35 hours a week, mostly at night after she took care of her daughters and husband and did other household chores.

At about 7:55 p.m. Tuesday, one who chose to

get money the easy way killed this concerned, conscientious woman in order, I suppose, to leave no witnesses. But, then, there was the camera. These are the words family and friends used to describe her: Friendly, happy, good personality, always smiling, talkative. You never left the store, they said, without her calling out, "Now have a good day."

Karen is 7 and Karla 5. Each wore blue jeans skirts and tops Thursday, and put shy smiles on their little faces as they offered handshakes. But a terrible look of loss filled their dark, misty eyes. Their mom's dead. Their family's torn apart. Because unchecked evil paid a visit to that crossroads store.

(October 12, 1990)

Cora Loves Living for Her Children

There are 81 reasons why Cora Emerson feels special on Mother's Day -- the 16 children she gave birth to and the 31 grandchildren and 34 great-grandchildren she got as a result.

It's crowded in Cora's cozy double wide mobile home on days like this, and the telephone rings a lot. She's not complaining. "My children's all I got to live for," she said, not smiling, but happy just the same.

Cora remembers being too busy keeping her family together to be happy on Mother's Day.

"We lived from house-to-house," she said of those years when she and her first husband, Alton "Pete" Smart, sharecropped farms and did other people's hard work for food to feed their children. At 85, Cora Emerson has had lung surgery, a mastectomy and now has trouble with her heart, but her eyes are clear and her memory sharp, and it's easy for her to dust off the years and remember when it began.

She was 15, Pete 20 when they married. He played in a band, and they met at a dance near Hazel Green. She was 16 when their first baby,

138

Paul, was born, but the little fellow only lived a week.

In all, she had eight single births and four sets of twins, astonishing since neither her family nor Pete's had twins. Eleven children are still alive. Judy was 18 months old when she died and Morris lived a week. James was 43 and Joan Pigg 36 when they died of cancer.

Wilma Best, Hilda Moss, Billie Smith, Leroy Smart and Roger Smart remain. So do twins Donnie and Ronnie Smart and Betty Wilbourn and Nettie Jobe. Also living are Marquita Isbell, Joan's twin, and June Lones, Judy's twin.

Only Hilda, who's in Michigan, isn't in the area, making it easier for Cora to be the mother and grandmother she wants to be.

Noting "all my babies was precious to me," Cora said "it just happened" that she and Pete had so many children. "The nights was long and cold," she said with an innocent smile. "I guess we could have watched TV if we'd had it."

Cora was "real happy" as a young mother. "I loved my husband with all of my heart. But we had a hard time."

Money and work were scarce. They often depended on family and friends. "I would ask for God to help me and to take care of my children and make things better for me," she said.

She and Pete Smart were married 52 years when he died in 1977. She married Frank Emerson in 1984, and although "I couldn't love a man better than I loved my first husband," the two years with Frank before his death in 1986 "was the happiest time of my life. It was all play and no work, and we went anywhere and everywhere."

Frank left her the mobile home, "the only home I ever had in my life."

Cora spends lots of time at garage sales ("I just like to prowl in other people's junk"), growing a garden with daughters Wilma and June or making her specialty, peach cobbler, on demand. She feels God still takes care of her and her children, not only on Mother's Day, but every other day, too.

(May 14, 1995)

If You Quit, You Might
Be an Invalid

The baby was a boy she named Ronald. He lived only 15 days. "But I did get to hold him in the hospital." What happened 52 years ago seems like yesterday to the baby's mother, Ruth. Even now her voice catches and her eyes water when talking about it.

"You lose one of your children, you never get over it, and if I'd had 15 it wouldn't take that one's place."

Ronald's middle name was Ruth's maiden name, and his last name was that of her first husband. The two of them were married four years when she got pregnant, and 10 years altogether. After Ronald died, "I cried all the time. I blamed everybody. We just drifted apart." After they divorced, she married John. They separated for two years, and then divorced in 1972 because, she said, "He couldn't be satisfied with one woman." She threw up her hands in mock alarm at mention of a third one and said, "I'm not interested now." A fellow from the Senior Center tried to court her. She declined. "I'm still attractive," she said with a wink and a smile, "although I don't look it today."

Ruth, who'll be 78 next month, lounged in her

hospital bed at home Friday and talked about life and politics. She couldn't have more babies after Ronald died, and talking about it still makes her want to cry. But she gets happier when talking about working in Washington, D.C., in the 1930s and '40s.

"I worked for the French government in their ordnance department," she said, then laughingly added, "I could have blown up all kinds of ships" in World War II. She and her second husband moved here in the mid-'60s when he went to work at the arsenal, and she lives in the house they bought then.

"I only got four more years and it's paid for," she said. The payments are $118 a month. She gets $325 a month in alimony from that husband and $132 a month from Social Security.

"I made a mistake when I was young and worked for the French, because they paid in cash, and I didn't get my Social Security credits," she explained.

She took her second husband to court and got alimony simply because "he ran off with some Hungarian woman" before their divorce and she wanted "to teach him a lesson."

What if he dies and the $325 a month stops? "If he dies I'll be out of luck," she answered. Then she smiled and said, "I don't let that worry me, there'll be some way."

As you might have noticed, Ruth doesn't hold

back. In fact, the only thing slowing her down is a bad hip which several operations didn't fix. A social worker from the Department of Human Resources comes two or three times a week and helps Ruth with bills, grocery list, the house and other things.

"She said she's gonna help me start walking next week," said Ruth with that smile on her face. "You got to figure out how to get around," she added, "unless you want to be an invalid." Slight pause. "I don't want to be an invalid."

Emphatically, "Why quit?" Then it's on to politics.

"Clinton's the best looking and the smartest of the Democrats, don't you think? But I like President Bush, too. And I loved John Kennedy -- go get me that book and let me show his picture, he was so handsome."

(March 1, 1992)

The Children Made It All Worthwhile

Dennis Bragg sleeps later. "I don't get up until 5:30 or 6 in the morning. That's not too early."

It's said with a genuine smile so it won't sound like he's being smart alecky.

Gladys Steger Bragg smiles, too, when admitting she doesn't get up when roosters crow, either.

They smile often, and should, having been married 58 happy years and being patriarch and matriarch of one of Madison County's last great farm families.

Son Allen, his wife Barbara, and the Braggs' daughter, Linda Kay Nord, make it easier for mom and pop to "sleep in" these days by running the farm's daily operations.

Linda Kay's husband, Kermit, a transplanted Minnesotan, helped until he returned to his first love, engineering.

But before hay balers and cotton picking machines, before children, and even before they had electricity, the elder Braggs were always up and going at daylight.

144

With land they leased and inherited, Dennis and Gladys started Bragg Farms in 1934 on the spot where their home still stands.

Dennis farmed with his father, Emmett, until he married Gladys in '34 and "it was time to get out."

Her father, Charlie Steger, owned a grocery store, a cotton gin and a grist mill between Meridianville and Hazel Green on what's now U.S. 231.

The empty store and abandoned gin are still there, and the Steger home, where Gladys' brother Steven lives, is across the highway about a quarter of a mile up Steger Road.

They met at a party, which Dennis said was "a nice party, not the rough type," courted for four years before marrying, and smilingly agreed it was because "we didn't have money for the license." When they moved to Grimwood Road in '35, the house was without electricity. They played bridge with friends by the light of kerosene lamps. They listened to battery-powered radio.

"I wasn't sorry to see those lamps retired," after they got electricity, Gladys said.

Added Dennis, "We don't want to see those "good old days" come back."

Dennis had two hired hands when he started. Now there are about 16 regulars and sometimes 24 or 25 when it's planting and gathering time. Bob Guthrie has worked on the farm since he was five years old, and Bob's father, Bill, worked for Dennis before that.

In those days, "I'd start in the fields about six or 6:30 and work until lunch, we called it dinner, and then work until sundown. When more land became available, if we had money, we'd buy. I never did consider doing anything else but farm." Gladys cooked, ran the house, raised flowers, and children. "I don't cook now," she said. "Too many people."

Allen Bragg plans the work now, but his father's out there every day helping make those plans succeed.

That might seem remarkable for a man 81 years old until you hear him explain why he still works: "Not too many people that retire and just quit and sit down live too much longer."

With that he smiled and said, "We're more proud of what our children have accomplished than what we've accomplished."

Then he motioned out the window toward farm buildings and crop land and said, "If we had all of that and the children didn't appreciate it, it wouldn't have meant much."

(April 5, 1992)

The Family Integrity's
at the Top of the List

KENNAMER COVE -- It was so hot the portable toilet felt like a sauna. It was so humid the chiggers that thrive in summer slumbered. But nothing weather or nature did dimmed the enthusiasm of "The Great American Family."

For the 69th consecutive year, the Kennamer Family Association met Saturday in the tin-roofed pavilion across the road from Mount Pisgah Baptist Church to renew friendships, take first looks at new babies and eulogize the dead.

Historic old Mount Pisgah, established in 1827, a dozen years after the first Kennamers settled here, still serves as a place of worship for those whose lives belong to this cove - and as many as 100,000 Kennamers are believed to have sprung from the original patriarch and matriarch. "When the Lord said `go out and multiply,' boy, those guys said `I know what you're talking about!' " is how Denton "Johnny" Kennamer explained the fruitfulness of his clan. He was standing in the family cemetery beside the tombstone of Hans and Rachel Kennamer, who settled here when this was still Indian territory.

Since then, 11 generations have lived in - and loved - Kennamer Cove, which is about halfway between the Jackson County town of Woodville and the Marshall County town of Grant.

Most of them eventually left to look for more land, but those who stayed, and those who registered with the Kennamer Family Association, are a powerful lobby that has beaten one attempt to change the cove's name and an effort to annex it.

Preserving the cove's integrity and its historical significance is high on the clan's list of musts, and those items are big reasons why the annual Kennamer family reunion is such a success.

Surrounded by several tables covered with food, those attending the reunion conduct business the old-fashioned way: Issues are discussed, then openly voted on by a show of hands.

They came from as far away as Utah this year to cast votes and to share in the fellowship.

By passing the hat, just over a thousand dollars was collected for the pot, which keeps the cemetery grass mowed, maintains the pavilion and takes care of other family matters.

Several books have chronicled them, including Woody Kelley's "The Great American Family," but no one knows the Kennamers like Wendell Page, whose family settled in the cove shortly after Hans and Rachel Kennamer.

Page knows that:

-- Hans B. Genheimer, born in 1620, was the patriarch who married the matriarch, Anna Marie Schmeltz, in Oppau, Germany,

-- Their son came to America so his son could escape poverty.

-- Genheimer was changed to Gennamer by customs agents writing down what they heard

-- Kennamer was the name that finally evolved.

Page said "the Kennamers still left in the cove are of the old bloodline who will hold on as long as they can."

You can count Audrey Kennamer Hall, 91, and Talmadge Kennamer, 83, who've attended all 69 family reunions, among them.

(August 5, 1997)

Not Famous -- Just a Pair
Who Made a Commitment

Lucille Ellett said it's no secret why her marriage has lasted so long. "Just love one another," she said. "If you love somebody, you're going to stay with them."

Through sad and happy times, and even at the beginning when they struggled so hard to stretch their few dollars, Lucille and James Ellett knew they'd be together until death parts them.

This afternoon, surrounded by family and friends at the East Huntsville Church of Christ where they've been members for 32 years, they celebrate their 65th wedding anniversary.

"They're nobody famous, just an elderly couple who've lived here all their lives," said one of their daughters, Gwen Boyd. But the way they've lived and how they overcame long odds spotlights a lost philosophy today's young marrieds need to be told about. He was 18, she was 14 when they met at preaching services in a Church Street community center. She was 15, he was 19 when they married.

Thus began the sustained journey from their August wedding day in 1932 until this afternoon's milestone celebration.

They first lived upstairs in a three-room house with his parents.

Lucille cooked on a wood-burning stove in their room. Both couples used an outhouse, a not-so-extraordinary occurrence then and the source of the old real estate joke: "three rooms and a path."

A big night out was going to a movie at the Elks Theater. Admission was a nickel. Most times they had to borrow the nickel from their grocer, who put it on their bill.

His first job was in a fabric mill for a dime an hour, 55 hours a week, while she stayed home to take care of the children. They eventually had nine, but three died in infancy and a fourth, Jerry, died in 1980.

The others are Ms. Boyd, Treva (Mrs. Jimmy) Mills, Brenda (Mrs. James) Wertz, Mike Ellett and Harold Ellett, whose wife is Connie. There are 13 grandchildren and 11 great-grandchildren (two more are on the way) who will hear again today how proud their parents and grandparents are of being the children of James and Lucille.

The five surviving Ellett siblings have never felt deprived. Brenda Wertz said "we always had a roof over our heads, we always had food on the table, we always had clothes to wear that were starched and ironed, and we always had a warm, loving home."

She and her brothers and sisters were "taught to respect other people and to work hard."

Work. When the youngest child, Gwen, started first grade, Lucille got a job in the school cafeteria and worked for 20 years. Only last February did James, a robust 84, retire as a Wal-Mart employee.

These days the Elletts grow vegetables in their spacious yard while James does woodwork in his spare time and Lucille continues doing what she always has loved doing - cook for her family. As for the future, Lucille's so sure her marriage to James will last she already has the cake picked out for her 70th wedding anniversary.

(August 17, 1997)

How Courage and Prayer
Won the Day

Birdhouses hang from almost every tree in their yard. He put several in neighbors' trees, too. Plus dozens more in the state park and around Burritt Museum on Monte Sano.

Clyde Hightower did this for two reasons. One, he wanted to keep bluebirds from becoming extinct. Two, he wanted his wife to continue her miraculous recovery.

He succeeded. Park officials said bluebirds aren't nearly as endangered now. And Betty Hightower has made it almost all the way back.

Tromping around the mountain with Clyde looking for places to hang birdhouses was the kind of therapy Betty needed. All that walking was healthy. Plus all those prayers. The Hightowers will tell you the prayers were healthiest of all.

"I am today what God wants me to be," Betty Hightower said Friday from her comfy chair in the cozy den of their home of almost 30 years.

In the spring of 1988, lots of people, including specialists, figured God wanted Betty dead. On a weekend trip to be with her father, she was stricken with what turned out to be massive strokes ... plural.

They rushed her to hospital via helicopter. "I knew it was serious then," Betty said. "When they came to school and showed us the helicopter, they said they only used it when things were serious." School was Davis Hills Elementary, where Betty was principal for 18 years. "They" were a Medflight crew which visited her students one day. So Betty figured the worst when she was put on the copter.

Then she slipped into a two-week coma and most folks wrote her off. But Clyde never left her side, and when the Hightowers' friends at Monte Sano Baptist Church began a prayer vigil, it spread across town, then to other spots in Alabama, and, eventually, to certain households in America.

In 1985, David Hightower, age 22, a senior in pharmacy at Auburn University, was home for a visit when he was involved in a car accident with a drunk driver. God had other plans that time, and David died. But He listened in the spring of 1988. Betty woke up. Clyde took over.

Before coming home, though, Betty said she remembered a doctor, who meant well, stood beside her and said, "Now you learn to be happy in that wheelchair." Betty said she said, "I'm gonna be happy ... but not in a blankty-blank wheelchair." Clyde, smiling, had to tell a story at this point.

"I knew she was going to be okay when our daughters (Kay Smith, Lynn Papp) were there on July 5th (1988) to feed her and she (Betty) grabbed the coffee cup and said, `I'll be damned if you're gonna feed me the rest of my life!' " Clyde added, "She is an assertive woman, and she didn't learn that in college." For her part, Betty said she never would have been able to "learn all over" without Clyde. He even taught her to fold clothes.

But the most important thing he did was teach her how to write, and it was easy. "She said she could just sign with an X, but I told her she'd never be able to use a charge card again," he explained.

Betty Hightower said she'd never have made it without Clyde. "He stood by me like I can't explain. If it had been him depending on me, I don't know if I could have done what he did." However, she does know this:"I can't give up because I can't let people down; they prayed for me all over this country."

(Jan. 26, 1992)

How They Became a Family

They looked at the situation from all sides and figured the only flaw in the plan was if they didn't follow their hearts.

So they not only agreed, they asked to take a baby only a few months old and in trouble. Nothing was wrong with its health, but something was wrong with its parents. They were neither married nor able to care for the child.

How the other couple became involved won't be shared today because they want to tell the story to the baby in their own way at the right time when it is older.

But the fact they got involved no doubt secured a better future for the baby without a home.

It's an old story, but the telling of it never grows stale, and this one does have a dramatic ending.

So the couple was allowed to bring the baby home, which must speak well of their character and such since they already have a baby and a teen-ager.

Bureaucracy sometimes can have a heart, though, and a judge signed papers giving the new baby a temporary home.

Of course, a period of time for everybody to live together to see if the thing worked was required.

Would the teen and the older baby accept the new one? They did, just like they were natural siblings. That's when the judge was asked to waive the one-year trial period, which he can do and which they thought he did.

A date was set for the final hearing and the excited family wanted to make it a real celebration. They put on their finest clothes, checked the teen out of school and planned to go to a restaurant for their first meal as a real family after the papers were signed.

Then thunder sounded and lightning struck. When they got to the judge's office his secretary told them the hearing was off. Why? they asked, and she said His Honor felt they needed to be together a full year before deciding.

"But he already waived the year!" they pleaded, at which point the secretary said he mustn't have because he had written "to be continued for a year" on the file.

Then the judge came to talk to them "and saw us," the father said, "standing there all dressed up with no place to go."

They were so torn up his wife "stood there with these big tears running down her cheeks," which the judge kept glancing at, but His Honor wouldn't budge.

So they left, heartbroken, and, since it was time to feed the babies, went on to a restaurant to eat, knowing the meal would be a sad one and not the happy one they'd planned.

But just as they sat down at a table, the husband's beeper went off. It was their lawyer with an important call. The judge had changed his mind and the hearing was on in 30 minutes.

Not believing it was happening, the family rushed back to the judge's chambers where they did, indeed, find His Honor ready and willing to accommodate.

Then the lawyer was late, but finally everyone was in place and the matter was settled.

The lawyer told the couple they'd probably get the final papers in a few days. The secretary whispered for them to wait there. When she returned, she presented the mother with the papers, signed and documented by the judge.

The child was theirs. They were still all dressed up and now really had someplace to go. So off they went for that long-delayed lunch.

(January 24, 1993)

VI. Liberators

On a Night With Wiley on My Mind

It took 'till the summer of my 51st year to get to Washington, D.C. I could have gone when my senior class in high school went, but for some reason I stayed home.

On Sunday, it was way after dark when we arrived, which I'm told is a fine time to see it, the reason being all the sights bathed in floodlights create a dramatic effect. It was dramatic, OK, seeing way yonder through trees on a hillside lights illuminating the roof of Lee House in Arlington National Cemetery where both hero and has-been are buried.

Looking around, I realized fortunes surely were made selling marble and granite to build all the monuments and museums, utility bills must be staggering for government offices big enough to float blimps in, and even Country-Comes-to-Town knew he was at the center of the universe when the Capitol and the White House suddenly sprang into view. The Washington Monument, tiny red light on its tip-top to scare airplanes away, looked like a bone-white spike, an enormous, solitary splinter of splendor sticking in the side of the night sky.

Off by himself was Thomas Jefferson. It's probably appropriate for him to stand over there alone thinking his brilliant thoughts.

If that great fashioner of public opinion was set loose in America today both sides and the middle would brand him a roaring radical. On the way to Washington white print on a green sign flashed a name as we crossed one of those interstate bridges you often miss. Bull Run, read the sign beside the stream. Just up the highway was the exit to Manassas.

Rebels named the battle after the village. Yankees named it after the stream. By either name, if Johnny Reb had kept chasing Yankees on the run that day in 1861, our Civil War might have been a short one with a different ending.

That was on my mind around elevenish Sunday night when after all these years I stood in the massive presence of Abraham Lincoln. On one wall was carved the Gettysburg Address, on another his second inaugural speech, and everywhere in that great hall where he sat echoed ghostly cries of victorious men, defeated men and freed men. The eyes in Lincoln's great, gaunt head followed me around his memorial, down its steps and across the street. Over there, on the other side in Constitution Gardens near the Reflecting Pool, they said I'd find the monument I most wanted to see.

The Vietnam Memorial near midnight was an awesome place to be. Soft floodlights helped reveal the 58,132 names grit-blasted into its black granite face. Bouquets of flowers and tiny American flags lay on the ground below it. There were three of us, but even at that late hour there were more. Three women, one elderly, linked arms and walked slowly past the names. A couple sat on a bench, the man's hands to his face, the woman's arms around his neck.

Wiley Hooks was stationed at Redstone Arsenal in the Public Information Office. He moonlighted for me in football season, calling in high school games. The Army sent him to Vietnam to do stories about local boys for hometown newspapers. I looked for him in that sacred place the other night and found him in section 10W, sixth line from the top.

(September 24, 1992)

161

Making Life Better
for Other People

Sunshine pouring through a window Wednesday brightened the second- floor study and matched Dr. Bessie Rivers Grayson's warm smile. "I remember, early-on, beginning to pick cotton," she said when asked to talk about growing up on her grandparents' farms outside the Marengo County town of Thomaston.

As a child, Bessie Rivers barely remembered her parents. When she was 5 months old, her mother died of illness. When she was 6 years old, her father was killed in an accident. Bessie and her sister Eula were raised by grandparents, aunts, uncles and practically everybody in Thomaston. "You have to soft-pedal with children now," she said,

but in that day everybody could help rear a child, unlike today when there is very little interference from the outside."

The woman who became a leading educator and humanitarian now says she knows she and Eula missed out on being told "only the things a mother and a father can tell you, but other than that we had a grand time." Bessie Grayson's story proves people of substance rise above mediocrity when someone guides them through their formative years. For Bessie, it was the Rivers family on her father's side and the Conner family on her mother's side.

Her mother's father, H.W. Conner, called "Poppa" by young Bessie, might have been her most positive influence.

Poppa was a religious man who paid his helpers at the end of every work day. He'd tell Bessie, Now they can go buy food and clothing if they need it." Poppa believed education was one of the keys to life," said Dr. Grayson," and he had a very strong work ethic." Those principles she learned from him later helped her have the spunk to teach classes at Alabama A&M in the morning then drive to Nashville that afternoon to attend Vanderbilt-Peabody and earn a doctorate in higher education.

Both sets of grandparents, including "Granddaddy" Sam Rivers, believed in sharing their resources. "They wanted us to visit the sick and to make life better for people." Despite the "separate but very unequal" school systems of her time and the "woeful tales" she could tell, Bessie got a bachelor's degree, a masters and a doctorate to fulfill her educational dreams. Armed with them, she spent her career with the idea she could make a difference. Along the way, she involved herself in efforts like Habitat for the Humanity and politics.

What happened to an uncle, William Napoleon Rivers, steered her into politics. He tried to help blacks in Mobile register to vote before there were civil rights laws and "almost lost his life when the authorities beat him up. I said from then on I would seek political office if one became available."

She has tried for council and School Board seats in Huntsville and for a spot in the Alabama legislature. "We did a lot of running and we never got elected," she said, smiling, "but we feel we made a contribution."

Retired since 1990, Dr. Bessie Rivers Grayson says she won't seek office again "although we would like to have served because we feel we could have brought some things to the forefront." That doesn't mean she won't be heard from again.

"I would like to be remembered as a person who shared my life with people in a variety of ways," she said with a smile, "and as a person who is never too busy to meet the needs of my fellow man in any way that I can."

(March 24, 1994)

He Decided Whose Fool He Was

The night of March 3, 1968, a ferocious fight broke out between a small group of U.S. Marines and a large North Vietnamese force. If daring helicopter pilots hadn't landed in rain and fog and evacuated the outnumbered Marines, not a single one would have survived.

Lt. Clebe McClary, a man who had believed he wouldn't get killed or hurt because he didn't smoke or drink and loved his wife, lost his left arm and left eye that night. But losing them helped him find his soul a few years later.

A native of Pawley's Island, S.C. (" We're famous for our rope hammocks."), McClary was a high school teacher and coach when he joined the Marines because he thought it was the right thing to do. He also thought the right thing to do was marry a girl named Deanna, who had been a student at the high school where he coached. They were married on Easter, 1967, but Clebe was too shy to kiss her "in front of all those people. Must have been 600. And Momma and Daddy were out there."

But he loved her so much the letters and tapes she sent not only helped him face combat, he said they gave him "something to live for" that dreadful night when hell came to visit his outfit on a jungle hill. It took almost three years for Clebe McClary to get back on his feet, and while he was getting there something happened that changed both his and Deanna's lives. They went to a crusade and, although both believed they were Christians, realized they weren't saved.

Clebe said when the preacher asked, "Whose fool are you? Are you a fool for Jesus? Or are you a fool for somebody else?" he knew whose fool he wanted to be.

Fast forward. Former Lt. McClary, who still looks trim in his Marine dress uniform, travels the land speaking to groups ranging from high schoolers to military officers. His American-as-apple-pie motivational messages are built around themes like pride, love and discipline.

This week he's at Whitesburg Baptist Church's "I Love America" celebration through Friday night. Sunday he'll be at "two little country churches in Tennessee." Next week he might be at a corporate outing anywhere.

Every six weeks he speaks to 800 officers at Maxwell Air Force Base's squadron leadership program, and this year has been invited to "welcome" the University of Alabama's football team back to fall practice.

"I love what I'm doing, but I don't love the travel," McClary said Tuesday afternoon.

Actually, he said travel's not bad, especially when Deanna is with him, "but she's home this week because we've still got a problem with our roof from (hurricane) Hugo and our daughter Tara has a job interview."

Their other daughter, Christa, serves right now as Clebe McClary Inc. office manager back on Pawley's Island, and all three of his women are proud of what Clebe is doing. McClary became a coach all those years ago because "all I ever wanted to do was influence young people in the right way." So now he has no other choice but to roam the land trying to do that. You see, losing an arm and an eye for his country taught him this: "You've got to bloom where you plant it."

(July 1, 1992)

The Legacy Still Points to Christ

Some say Dr. Martin Luther King Jr. predicted his death in a passionate sermon the night before. He said he'd been to the mountaintop, and had seen the promised land. He was killed the next day on the balcony of a Memphis motel. King died April 4, 1968, and one of those floored by the catastrophe was a young preacher named Julius Edward Scruggs.

Eight years earlier, while the civil rights movement was still a sapling, teen-ager Scruggs became influenced by King's peaceful but firm leadership. Scruggs was 18 and attending American Baptist College in Nashville in 1960 when he heeded the call to protest unrighteous treatment. Wary, but not afraid of the consequences, he joined the lunch counter sit-ins sweeping the South. The protests continued through 1961, and so did Scruggs, who was by then a hardened veteran of the civil rights movement at 19.

Looking back at those tumultuous times, which seem like only yesterday but happened almost 40 years ago, the college boy who grew to be a man said: "I just thought to have segregated drinking fountains and places where we couldn't eat together was both unfortunate and un-Christlike." Scruggs has dignified the pulpit at First Baptist Church for 20 years, and King's influence still rings clearly in the message he delivers.

In fact, when he got his doctorate from Vanderbilt University in 1975, he wrote his dissertation about King. Scruggs was bound to preach. His father, Earl Scruggs Sr., was the pastor of churches in Limestone, Morgan and Madison counties. His grandfather, Julius Caesar Scruggs, pastored in Elkton, Tenn., and taught school in Madison County.

Born in Giles County, Tenn., Scruggs started first grade in Madison County - and began preaching at 17. He was already preaching when he went to preacher school. On this King holiday weekend, pastor Scruggs shared some thoughts on the subject.

If King lived today, he said, "I think he would emphasize again what he wrote in the book `Chaos and Community,' that the globe is a community house and we all have to live in it together, Easterner and Westerner, Jew and Gentile, or we will die fools."

He said church consciousness "has been heightened with regard to racial injustice. Some corrections and strides have been made from within and without the church. However, I think we've come to a point in America where we need to reawaken our consciousness about brotherhood and sisterhood."

Most important, Dr. Scruggs feels King's "life and legacy reminds us we need to be serious about the redemptive love as practiced by Jesus Christ, our model, our savior and our Lord."

(January 19, 1997)

The Reason One Veteran
Was Riding in a Parade

A feeling of foreboding covered John Barnacle
that frosty morning of March 17, 1944, as he
crammed into his position beneath the plane. He
was just 5 feet 6 inches tall and weighed 145
pounds, but the ball-turret gun post was so
cramped he couldn't wear his flak jacket and fit
inside.

Then True Love was airborne, headed to
Austria from Italy on another long and dangerous
bombing run. True Love was the name of the F-24
Liberator that Barnacle and 10 other crew
members were flying. It was the airplane's first
mission since it had been repaired after being shot
to pieces coming back from another run weeks
before.

The crew had been fortunate then, but
Barnacle, a 24-year-old staff sergeant from
Massachusetts, couldn't shake his bad feeling as
the plane roared toward Vienna. His fears were not
unfounded; German ground guns mortally
wounded the plane high above Yugoslavia.

171

The plane's pilot, 1st Lt. Reaford C. McCraw, ordered his crew to bail out, held the plane steady while the others jumped, then went down with the craft. Barnacle landed in the rugged mountains of Bosnia, hurting his back and head when he hit ground. All he had for help was a compass about the size of a quarter. He walked toward the setting sun, not knowing where the path would lead.

He had no food for 21 days. He put snow in his mouth and let it melt for drinking water. He eluded capture several times by hiding behind boulders and among trees that dotted the rugged terrain. Once, when he despaired most, he fell to his knees in the snow and prayed for God's help. He felt someone beside him at once. He never saw this presence, but he thinks it was an angel.

Finally, a Yugoslav partisan found him, put him over his shoulder like a sack and took him to where some British soldiers were. But before doing that, he took him to the True Love crash site. There, in that sacred place, John Barnacle gave 1st Lt. McCraw a Christian burial.

Barnacle weighed 80 pounds when he got back to Italy. He was a basket case, mentally and physically. He had flown 19 missions and wanted to continue, but his superiors said no. He spent almost the next 50 years trying to get a Silver Cross for McCraw. He was rebuffed by several U.S. senators and two presidents. In the end, the only award the heroic pilot received was a Purple Heart.

John Barnacle is 78 and lives from day to day. He doesn't look ahead to tomorrow because he has cancer in his prostate and his lungs. But he rode in the military parade downtown this morning because he wants us to realize what Veterans Day is supposed to be.

"It's to honor the memory of people like my pilot," he said. "It's to remember the sacrifice" of the 1,505 men in his bomber group alone who died in World War II.

"We were flying for duty and love of country," the old Air Corps gunner said, tears rising in his eyes.

"We were proud to be American patriots."

(November 11, 1997)

A Glorious Outcome for a Hero and His Champion

How many people have you met who absolutely put so much passion into a cause it threatened to consume them? How many people have you met who willingly aggravated family members, provoked entire government agencies and made a nuisance of themselves to all others in order to reach a noble goal? How many people have you met who were told "no" for 50 years but just wouldn't listen?

John Barnacle was an Air Force staff sergeant and gunner in a bomber named "True Love," which was shot to pieces twice during bombing runs in World War II. The first time, the True Love pilot, 1st Lt. Reaford McCraw, managed to escape packs of attacking German fighters by using daring dives and heart-stopping spins before finally skimming his crippled craft just above the waves of the Adriatic Sea to safety.

German pilots raked True Love for 90 long and unmerciful minutes that day before the tattered bomber made it to base in Italy, but because of the pilot's cool actions, none of the crew was killed. McCraw was nominated for the Silver Star and the Distinguished Flying Cross after that engagement in February of 1944.

A month later, when bullet holes in their craft had been repaired, McCraw and his crew were on another bombing run when True Love was hit by ground fire. This time the plane was mortally wounded. Coolly, McCraw kept it aloft until his crew bailed out. But he could not escape. He went down with True Love on March 17, 1944.

Later, John Barnacle returned to that part of Yugoslavia where the plane crashed, found the pilot's body and, helped by partisans, gave the heroic man a Christian burial. Then Barnacle's Quixote-like quest began.

Determined to make sure the medal nominations didn't fall through the cracks because the pilot was dead, he started searching for McCraw's family members to enlist their help. Barnacle knew the pilot was originally from Oklahoma, had lived in Arkansas and was believed to have relatives in Texas, but the trail grew cooler as the years rolled by.

Meanwhile, he fired off a constant barrage of letters to the military, the federal government and local and national politicians. He badgered the press to keep printing his story. Frankly, he worried some people to death.

Thursday, in the Commanding General's

Conference Room of the U.S. Army Aviation and Missile Command at Redstone Arsenal, the old staff sergeant's crusade came to a glorious end. With a brother and sister from Texas in attendance, 1st Lt. Reaford McCraw was awarded his Distinguished Flying Cross posthumously in an emotional ceremony held 54 years after he unselfishly saved his crew.

John Barnacle, an old man fighting cancer, sat ramrod straight in his chair as the award was presented, his mind most likely on the day another man died to save him.

Only when the moment was over and the importance of all he had done had pressed its way into his heart did he cry.

(November 15, 1998)

He Surely Was a Man to Emulate

Maybe they'll play one of the songs or read one of the poems L.C. Jamar wrote. Maybe they'll sing "Angels Will Come With Christ" or recite "O Lord Our Great Creator." It'll be appropriate if the funeral today of this unique and gifted man is celebrated with words of his own invention.

L.C. Jamar died Tuesday. He was 91. Those who knew him know God surely had a purpose in providing such longevity. He was a man for all seasons, and his death leaves a void no t only in the black community, but the whole community. Somebody else said this a long time ago, but it applies to the man they bury today: He was a credit to his race, the human race.

L.C. Jamar was educator, preacher, writer, editor, and newspaper owner in his long and storied life. He provided a voice and a platform for blacks in the Tennessee Valley when they had neither. Yet he gathered a multitude of friends of every color, a "rainbow coalition" before the term became fashionable.

One of those friends, the Rev. L.G. Fields,

fondly remembers "the many long years I had contact with him." Fields, who'll be 100 years old next February, recalled how Professor Jamar asked him to write a weekly sermon in his newspapers, first the Mirror and then The Weekly News. Fields had 550 of those sermons published in Jamar's papers.

"I encouraged him to stay in school, and it turned out to be a great thing for him," he said. It turned out to be great for the black community, too, because L.C. Jamar served 44 years as teacher and principal in county schools, and as far back as 1931 was trying to get a supervisor "of colored schools" in the county.

The Rev. Julius Scruggs. pastor of First Baptist Church, pointedly declared Professor Jamar to be "a pioneer in Journalism that pertained to the black community. He was a fine and outstanding citizen of this entire community. He will be missed". Superintendents of education and sheriffs of this county were among his closest friends. In fact, when he retired from education, the issue of The Weekly News printed on that occasion was filled with congratulatory advertisements from white-owned businesses.

He had that kind of association with an effect on all of Huntsville. In 1983, when he was 83, Jamar played pioneer again when he merged The Weekly News with Speakin' Out' News of Decatur to form one of the largest black-circulation publications in Alabama. He wrote many songs which were recorded, and several poems, preached, sold insurance and ran for public office twice.

Perhaps his greatest salute came from a member of the family, grandson Ronald Jamar, banquet manager of the Huntsville Hilton and Towers. "He showed me the value of hard work," young Jamar said. "He was always an inspiration in my spiritual life, and in the last few months when I'd read the Bible to him, he'd call me "preacher."

But L.C. Jamar's finest legacy can be found in these words by his grandson; "We all search for someone to emulate. I looked to Dr.Martin Luther King and to John and Robert Kennedy. But I really didn't have to search that far. I had L.C. Jamar."

(June 9, 1991)

Cashin: Remembering
a Woman of Conviction

If words can paint a picture of a person's personality, tributes offered at Joan Cashin's memorial service produced a portrait of the perfect pioneer. And in the early struggle for civil rights, a pioneer is what she was.

Standing beside her husband, Dr. John Cashin, in the turbulent early 1960s, Mrs. Cashin helped pioneer the cause of equality by taking to Huntsville's streets in non-violent civil disobedience.

During the time she and a coalition of local black leaders staged sit-ins which led to the desegregation of public drinking fountains and rest rooms here in 1962, she proudly was arrested while holding her four-month-old daughter, Sheryll, in her arms.

Later, she waged a war on poverty by helping low income families for almost 25 years as supervisor of community services for the Community Action Agency of Huntsville and Madison County.

Those were among the moments recalled when family and friends gathered Thursday at the First Missionary Baptist Church to reflect on the life of Joan Carpenter Cashin, who died last Saturday at the age of 61. Edwin Hill, who worked with her for almost 20 years at CAA, called Mrs. Cashin an "enlightened and intelligent person who was totally committed to the mission of eliminating poverty in the midst of plenty."

Elder E.C. Ward said she was "a woman of conviction and a woman who was loyal to her duty. Above all, she was a Christian."

In his enthusiastic, eloquent eulogy, the Rev. Dr. Henry Bradford Jr., pastor of the Church Street Cumberland Presbyterian Church in America, said "all things are possible if you believe in God . . . and that's the kind of spirit Joan Cashin had."

She was "a humanitarian at heart who was affected by an inescapable desire to do something for others," said the pastor, who noted she was not motivated by awards or commendations but saw suffering and sadness and tried to heal it. Bradford said she was "feminine, but not necessarily a feminist," was "given to grace and charm," and was a woman who "lived a life of genuine service." But, he testified, she was first and foremost "an animated antagonist of racism and an active advocate of its abolishment."

In his own tribute to his fallen wife, John Cashin reminisced about their life together, about how proud they were of their three children, John Marcus, Carroll and Sheryll, and about how "Joan cared enough about me and loved me enough to come to Alabama and help bear my burdens" after they married.

He said he promised his wife "on her death bed" he would finish the job of bringing about the concepts of racial and financial equality which the two of them started working toward almost 40 years ago.

Very few young blacks attended the memorial service, but their generations should be aware of the legacy left by civil rights pioneers such as Joan C. Cashin, who once went to jail for her convictions.

(September 7, 1997)

His Aching Heart Has Been Eased

There was a small story in Saturday's paper headlined "Vietnam won't hinder search." He probably would have clipped it and mailed it to me with more of his type-written thoughts.

In the years after I left the city desk and started writing a column, we often shared his feelings about a multitude of things. The Vietnam war and everything patriotic headed the list. He would have been happy with Saturday's brief about Vietnam helping American investigators sent to solve the puzzle of missing American servicemen.

He would also have been suspicious. He and his contemporaries had hearts broken and hopes dashed too many times to believe the suspects would suddenly tell the truth or help solve the mystery.

That's what he'd have written in his note if he had clipped Saturday's story and sent it to me. His messages weren't all that frequent, which is one reason I paid attention when they arrived. He wrote or called to compliment my columns favorable to the military, especially those about

Vietnam veterans.

He was a Vietnam vet and damned proud of it. He also thought the majority wrongly condemned him and his peers for being there. "We were soldiers doing what soldiers are told to do," he once exclaimed.

I believe his post-Vietnam experiences kept him from being as good of a journalist as he could have become because he read conspiracy into many things. Later, when we lunched together, or when I read his letters, I learned why he felt that way, and the learning let me listen with lots more patience.

Our correspondences revealed a contradiction: He was unhappy because of how he perceived America treated Vietnam vets, yet was hopeful his friends and neighbors and every stranger he met would one day accept what had been done. He telephoned me and cried after the Vietnam memorial in Washington was dedicated.

He telephoned me and laughed like a little boy while telling me he and some other Vietnam vets had been invited to march in a parade. He wore his red T-shirt with yellow lettering every chance he got, and talked about what they meant more often than that.

"Vietnam Veterans of America." Those words on those shirts meant something special to him, because he felt in his heart his buddies were something special.

184

He never talked about his experiences in Vietnam. Like the journalist he later became, his stories were about other men. He seemed to grieve for them more than he grieved for himself, a fault which haunted him most of the time.

He couldn't understand why so many people seemed to be mad at his buddies, who had only gone and done what "Uncle" had ordered them to do.

He mailed me pictures he clipped out of the paper of children waving American flags at Fourth of July parades and wrote "Praise God!" or "Ain't This Great!"

Then he mailed me articles where somebody said Vietnam was a disgrace and his mood would be dark and his words would be those of a hurting man.

He dealt with his heartache in his own way, mostly in solitude, and although I knew a little, I didn't know what was in his heart of hearts. Vietnam can't hurt John Park anymore. He was buried Saturday. The cause of death could have been listed as life.

(April 26, 1992)

It's Easier to Laugh About It Now

Slender William Rush, wearing white casual clothes and with a multi-colored Hawaiian lei around his neck, grins impishly at laughter caused by the cartoon he shows.

In it, one fellow says to another while a third sits at a table with a drink in his hand. ""Harry likes to remember Pearl Harbor. He gets bombed every night."

Rush gets away with it because of membership in an exclusive society: Pearl Harbor Survivors Association Inc.

Thursday afternoon, Rush is busy. As Pearl Harbor Survivors' sixth district director, he alternately meets the press and greets members from eight Southeastern states in town for the group's convention. High-voltage nervous energy carries him.

Forty-nine years after Dec. 7, 1941, Rush and his mates can laugh at the cartoon. On the morning of the infamous event, things were more somber. But Rush remembers not being afraid then. "I didn't get scared until we sailed into open waters, and it was dark, hunting the Japanese.

He was 18, a radio operator on the light cruiser U.S.S. Phoenix when the first wave of Japanese planes and submarines attacked at 7:55 a.m. The Phoenix was anchored one ship from the Arizona, whose hulk with over 1,000 bodies aboard rests at the bottom of Pearl Harbor as a monument today. Rush says, "I was just a kid from Alabama, and I was so green I was envious other ships got hit and we didn't"

He smiles, "I'm not now."

Then he tells about the Phoenix's interesting life.

"We were in nine battles, never took a hit and only had two men killed. After the war, Truman (President Harry S.) sold her to Argentina. They renamed her the General Belgrano. We were negotiating to buy her back when the British sunk her in the Falklands War and killed 358 men."

The plan was to anchor her at Pearl near the Arizona. "Phoenix was the lucky ship, Arizona the unlucky. Since she was named for the city from the same state, it was to be a tribute. Phoenix rising from the ashes, you know."

The cartoon reminds Rush of how Pearl Harbor Survivors began. "It was 1958 and six guys who were in a bar in Los Angeles and decided to form a club. The next time they met, eight more guys joined. It took off from there."

There are 11,000 survivors, male and female,

still accounted for. The oldest is George Bauer, 79, of Citronelle, Ala. The youngest are now 67, except, Rush says, "for one guy somewhere who claims he lied about his age and was 15 when he joined the service."

Jesse Sisk of Manchester, Tenn., was also on the Phoenix. The two men remember standing on deck and watching bodies being piled up in the village of Aiea after the attack. More than 2,400 American service men and women died in the first 55-minute assault and the shorter second one.

Each man has dealt with those frightful minutes of Dec. 7, 1941, in different ways. Rush retired in 1962 rather than be stationed in Japan, although, he says, "I have no hate in my heart." Sisk was stationed in Japan for two years after the war and found the people "to be trustworthy and honest." But he did trade for a new American-made car to come to this reunion.

Next year, the national reunion will be held in Hawaii to mark the 50th anniversary of Pearl Harbor.

Rush, who has been back several times, says it will be emotional. "When you stand there and face the Arizona and hear them sing those sad Hawaiian songs, it's magnificent. You get goose pimples."

He wipes tears from his eyes.

(May 25, 1990)

VII. Rambling Thoughts

They Sure Have Great Acoustics

The groom dropped the ring, not me.

Two bridesmaids, the flower girl and a parson are my witnesses.

The bride will also confirm the truth, since it was her finger he was about to slip the ring on when he dropped it.

Yet rumormongers and gossips said I was guilty, news which had spread like wildfire through the reception hall.

Common sense tells you the groom did it. He used to be a quarterback. Everybody knows there's not a worse group of fumblers than they.

You had to be there to appreciate it. I'll tell the parishioners one thing, their church has wonderful acoustics. Sounded like two cymbals being banged together when that sucker hit the floor.

He got one of those lucky bounces and it came right back to him, but for a split second I thought it was headed for the aisle.

Gossips and rumormongers blamed me because I wrote something Friday about hoping I didn't lose the ring. The groom blamed the gloves he had to wear. I prefer his version, which happened to be the truth.

Maybe I could have predicted it would happen. He fussed for several minutes before the ceremony about having to wear gloves. "They're slick," he said, but I figured it was only because he was so nervous he was sweating like a horse.

This was when he and I were in a little room next to the sanctuary waiting for the parson. There was a wall phone in the room. Hoping to ease his tension, I casually mentioned maybe the governor would call and give him a reprieve. Just before the organ signaled the beginning, he looked at me and said, "I don't think the governor's gonna call."

Well, if he'd had better coaching, he might not have fumbled at the most crucial moment of his life. (I'm still amazed at how much noise that little ring made.) Although some blamed me, it actually was the fault of all the men for whom he played football, baseball and basketball.

They know who they are, so there's no use in naming names. A couple of them were there, and they know in their hearts who really dropped the ring. The padre will tell you I smoothly transferred that ring to his hands, and it was when he told the groom to slip it on his bride's finger that the mishap took place.

If it had been a baseball game, the official scorer would have scored it "E Groom."

However, the boy recovered nicely, even managing to mutter "Fumble!" on the way to the floor to cover it.

Sure I laughed. The preacher laughed. Everybody in the building laughed.

But I'll not take the blame. I guarded that ring with my life all night long. The first thing I did Saturday morning was make sure it was where I put it Friday night.

No ring in the history of matrimony has ever had such a fuss made about it.

After all of that, it's hard to believe anybody'd think I let it fall to the floor.

The groom dropped the ring, not me.

Probably because he played quarterback, and we all know those people invented the fumble.

I'm glad it's over. The guy who dreamed up tuxedos should have to wear one. White gloves, too. But I wish we'd had a video and sound track of the ceremony.

If we had, we could enter it in one of those home video contests and maybe win money. And I could rest my case about who dropped what.

(May 17, 1992)

Why Didn't the Soldiers Get a Bonus?

You've got to feel sorry for professional athletes.

No matter how much money they make, it's not enough.

And in feeling sorry, you don't have to dig any deeper than Sunday's Super Bowl between Washington and Buffalo.

Several days before the game, reporters looking for stories pointed out to Buffalo quarterback Jim Kelly that the $36,000 each member of the winning team would get was less than he got for each regular season game.

Kelly, you see, has a contract worth millions of dollars over several seasons. Broken down on a per-game basis, his paychecks look quite handsome, if not bizarre.

So when the ink-stained wretches told Kelly what he'd get if his team won Sunday, he replied, "Yeah, sucks, doesn't it?"

And that's why I feel sorry for professional athletes.

I mean, you can't expect a guy to take a cut in pay when he's playing for the world's championship, can you?

Since Kelly's team didn't win, you could say he practically played for nothing.

The indignity of getting thumped in full view of millions thanks to television and getting paid only 20 or so thousand!

I'll bet if he and his mates knew they were only gonna make that much for a single game they'd have gotten mad enough to think about getting real jobs.

Except I don't know where they'd get real jobs paying what they make in a year, or even what poor old Buffalo's losers had to take Sunday.

Not counting coaches, trainers and equipment men, who all get a share of the loot, there are 45 players on a pro football team. This means Washington's players split about $1,620,000.

The only jobs I know with bonus money like that at the end of the year are either chairmanships of automobile companies or heads of drug cartels, and I believe all those posts are currently filled.

Actually, I suppose Kelly does have a gripe. His career's at stake every time the ball's snapped. One bad lick and it's goodbye high life, hello television announcer's booth. Kelly could also have been thinking about the fact that baseball players got about 80-grand for the World Series, and we all know it's easier to get hurt playing football. But, of course, the baseballers do have to play at least four games and possibly seven before going to the bank.

Yet if footballers feel they should be paid more because of chancing irreparable maiming, then employees exposed to danger in other lines of work should be taken care of, too. Uncle Sam's soldiers quickly come to mind, for instance. We all know our boys and girls in combat made quick work of Iraq. It was sort of like Sunday's Super Bowl, with our soldiers playing the role of Washington.

Since the war was shown on television, just like the Super Bowl, why weren't our troops treated like pro athletes and allowed to share in a pool of bonus money?

Well, I guess if television could have justified stopping the war every 10 minutes to show five minutes worth of commercials there'd have been a possibility. Since it couldn't be justified, our soldiers just had to make do with their regular pay.

Which -- and I'm sure Jim Kelly would be the first to agree -- sucks. But, then, throwing footballs, hitting baseballs and shooting basketballs is more romantic than those dirty, bloody, deadly wars.

(January 28, 1992)

I'd Rather Do Anything
Than That

I wouldn't want to be a newspaper headline writer these days.

Seems like all they deal with are death, pestilence, famine and disease.

Unless it's graft, theft, lying and greed.

Or raping, abusing, hating and cheating.

These things have always been around, but not quite in the quantities we have today.

The reason it seems like there's more is because we now have instant communication with the world.

Which means every wire service can carry every piece of bad news happening anywhere in the known world. Somebody at the paper has to write headlines on those stories, and I'm glad it's not me because I know how bad I'd feel at the end of the day.

I'd rather go back to being sports editor and putting up with nasty letters and phone calls from Auburn and Alabama fans than being a headline writer.

-- A headline writer is:

---A messenger who always gets shot.

-- A waiter who brings the bill.

-- A fly in the soup.

-- A shoelace that always breaks.

--A black-sheep brother.

--A kid who's always the last one chosen.

In other words, nothing real good.

But only because the world has turned out to be such a rotten place.

Well, it was always rotten, but now it's easier to put the rotten together. I've only recently realized why the best headline writers I ever knew were hard drinkers. If I had to sit there every day and write headlines they have to write, I'd be a hard drinker, too.

I hope those who write headlines now don't ignore spouses or fuss at children when they get home, but it won't surprise me if they do. I'd rather be a mortician or a politician. Come to think of it, I imagine morticians and politicians sleep sounder than headline writers. Most people count sheep when they sleep, but I suspect headline writers count starving babies in Ethiopia.

Why not? They're exposed to that kind of thing every day. Plus the number of senseless murders and brainless assaults on our streets. Wouldn't it be great if headline writers got to write good stuff instead of bad stuff most of the time?

Here are some headlines I bet they'd like to write, but we probably won't ever get to see:

"Local doctors burn cancer hospital to ground after cure for disease found"

"No robberies reported anywhere for two months"

"Divorce placed on endangered species list"

"Coalition of teen gangs awarded Volunteer of Year award; youths cited for anti-crime, anti-drug awareness programs"

"Poll shows citizens back police 100 percent"

"NCAA report says every college athletic program in America is clean"

"Racism, sexism, jingoism and most every other kind of ism said to be on endangered species list"

"A worldwide wonder: America's students and cars rated No. 1 around the globe"

"Cops say breathalyzer a thing of the past because nobody drives drunk anymore"

"Recession and inflation have become only words in the dictionary"

"Malls are so safe after dark mothers take children shopping with them"

"No bad news today; headline writers seen smiling for first time in two decades" So when you scan the paper today, please think kindly of headline writers.

They'd like to write about good things. Honest they would.

(January 21, 1992)

Wait'll They Meet
Sack and Pillage

There goes the neighborhood. It's bad enough they weasled around and have the Rocket City Marathon coming past my front door Saturday morning, they plan a warmup jog past it Friday night. Wait'll my councilman has another fireside chat.

If those guys who run the Huntsville Track Club were really my friends, they'd have inverted the course so I'd be near the finish instead of the start.

But, no, they think they've kept me from making a buck by positioning my place in the first 20 minutes of the race. Even if it's warm, nobody will want cold beer less than two miles into the course.

They made sure when runners are hot, tired, sweaty and thirsty they'll be way down in southeast Huntsville.

I'll bet dollars to doughnuts Tinsley, Hillis, Oaks and that crowd already have concession stands manned by wives, sons and daughters planned for strategic spots.

Well, I don't intend to take it lying in bed. In

198

fact, I plan to get up and sell coffee to spectators. So let me invite all you moms, dads, wives, husbands, children, and sweethearts of marathoners to my front yard Saturday morning for breakfast.

In honor of this big event, as a one-time special I'll offer coffee, a vanilla wafer with peanut butter on it, and a place to stand by the curb and cheer for only $5 a head.

For competitors, here's another can't miss deal: The low, low price of $15 will get you a secret minivan ride down Steele Street and up East Clinton to the corner of Calhoun, where you will skip four blocks and 600 runners. How can this be accomplished? Easy. When you get in front of my house, pretend you sprained an ankle and have to use my phone to call a doctor, then we sneak out the back door and, whisk, away we go. It'll be simple. A flashing sign in my yard will say, "Attention Cheaters! This is it!" But I hope you've heard about cash and carry. No cash, no carry.

Meanwhile, there must be ways to make a buck with that Friday afternoon jogging deal.

I read where it's going to be called the Historic Huntsville Run. The idea is to let visiting marathoners loosen up with a jogging tour of the Old Town and Twickenham districts.

Let's see, now, what other old ruins besides my own here are worth seeing? Hey, I've got an idea. I read where Friday's start is 4 p.m. and it might include a hundred runners. If it's a regular day on Holmes Avenue East, the going-home traffic will be ripping around the corners of Lincoln and Monroe about then, and if joggers are in the street those cars will scare the .... out of them. I can charge $1 each to come in and use my toilet, towels a quarter extra, of course.

While there, some of them might want to pre-sign for the minivan ride next morning, or even buy assigned spectator spots for a loved one. I think funeral homes call that pre-planning.

Anyway, my humble little block on Holmes Avenue East anxiously awaits Saturday's big event.

What a thrill! What an honor! What time will it be before we can get cars out of driveways?

One last item. If you're gonna watch from my yard, be early. You won't want to miss what happens when the first runners race past.

My neighbor lets his two dogs out to do their business about that time. Their names are Sack and Pillage. They bite ankles.

(January 12, 1992)

Could Be She Was
the Circus Lady

Mostly, I throw junk mail in the trash can at the post office without opening it. But the other day came this letter I couldn't ignore. The return address said it was from Roxanna.

The reason I opened it was because I thought it was from that big-chested woman who runs out on the field and gives ballplayers a kiss. Then I remembered her name is Morganna. Since I'd already torn open the envelope, I figured, what the heck. I'll see what it is.

Turns out I'm Roxanna's "dear friend," although, since she lives in Virginia, I can't, for the life of me, remember where we met. Anyway, Roxanna (she didn't say Miss, Mrs., or Ms.) Says according to the stars, "great and exciting things could soon be on the way." Which is sort of like saying I could live to be 100.

However, it seems Roxanna "has helped thousands across America gain incredible insights" through her special astrological reports. Well, yeah, I thought , here it comes now; send X number of dollars and she'll put me on a special mailing list reserved for her best friends.

But, no. Roxanna never mentioned a fee in her six or seven-page epistle. Did, in fact, encourage me to simply mail back a "confidential" client survey and she'd send a free gift. It wasn't a hard survey, either. Only several questions to be answered yes or no. Things like did I want to improve my love life, get filthy rich, or both. Well, now, let me think.

Okay, Roxanna, I do, I do, I do, I do! I'll fill in that survey, put it in the handy return envelope, lick the stamp, and fire it back to you so I can get my wires, I mean stars, crossed, and also my mysterious free gift. What could it be? An appearance on Star Search? A Huntsville Stars T-shirt?

Then, oops, in small print, but not too small, at the bottom of the yes and no questions and answers survey, I noticed two little boxes to mark. One said, "Enclosed is my check for $19.95 (plus $2.05 for first class shipping and handling. Maryland residents please add 5 percent sales tax) made payable to Roxanna. This is payment in full for the "Progressive Revelations Forecast." The other said, "Please charge my Visa or MasterCard as follows:"

Tell me where these people come from? Naw, tell me how they get my post office box number? Dear friend my hind end. It wasn't addressed to "Bill," or even "William." It was sent to "W."

Easterling. Hey, I haven't been called "W" since dad picked that letter out when I was born and told mom the rest of the name was up to her, but he thought she should use a vowel or two.

How can a gift be free if it's going to cost $22? Isn't that false advertising? Can't I sue? Well, that ripped it for me, and I can tell Roxanna she's not going to get a cent. Made me madder than I already was when I realized the letter wasn't from Morganna.

I did have my palm read once at a circus. The lady said I had a long life line and fortune was in my future. She only charged 50 cents. She had a towel tied on her head and earrings down to her shoulders.

Now that I remember, she did say, "Sit down, my dear friend." You don't think....

(April 12, 1991)

You Can See the Summers
of Yesterday From Here

MULBERRY, Tenn. -- Early in the afternoon on the first day of my favorite season, Mulberry lies like a lazy turtle on a log, quiet and unmoving, hoping no one comes along to startle it.

On a rectangle of ground in the center of the hamlet is the statue of a man holding a gun and wearing a uniform, and chiseled in the granite below him are these words:

"In grateful remembrance of the 300 Confederate unconquered soldiers who went out from Mulberry."

Donated and erected by the United Daughters of the Confederacy, the statue is bordered on three sides by places of worship, Baptist, Methodist and Church of Christ, all made of boards painted white and all bearing the village name.

Within the periphery of the Southern soldier's vision is a small brick post office, a car with the words State Trooper painted on it parked in front of a satellite outpost, and the rotting frame of a long-gone general store.

Not a soul is to be seen here but, a block away, an old fellow shelling peas on his porch never

204

looks as a strange car slowly cruises his neighborhood.

Next door, though, an old woman in a rocking chair has come outside to catch a cool breeze - her hose are rolled down to her ankles and her dress is pulled up to her knees - and she gives a slight wave.

There are flower beds in the front yards and old sheds with rusted tin roofs in the back yards of Mulberry. The creek beside it bears the name from which the hamlet sprang. Or is it the other way around?

Which came first, creek or village, is not important on the first day of the new season; the Queen Anne's Lace along both sides of Highway 50 as it passes this hidden hamlet already has me thinking of the summers of my youth.

This is the kind of village my family lives in when my tongue first tastes, my nose first smells and my eyes first see summer.

My friends and I eat and sleep in a place just like this, and we swim in a nearby stream just like Mulberry Creek. There is a deep spot in our creek we call "the swimmin' hole." We throw our clothes in a pile and swim naked in the warm, green water.

We tie a rope to a tree and play Tarzan, swinging far out over the creek, then yelling as loud as we can, like the Ape Man does in the movies, as we plunge into the water below.

When we grow weary, we go pick blackberries and eat them until our fingers turn purple and our stomachs ache.

We need no watch to tell us when it's time to go, for someone's mother is always cooking fried chicken for supper and the smell of it is so deliciously overpowering the aroma drags us home.

In case we forgot to do some chore we were supposed to do before we left, we pick wildflowers to present to our mothers when we get home. We put the bouquets in Mason jars, water them and set them on the counter in her kitchen, right next to the stove. It makes a very nice arrangement, and almost always earns an extra slice of apple pie for dessert.

I hear we return to our childhood when we grow old.

On Monday, the first day of summer, 1999, in this unhurried village hiding in the rolling hills of Tennessee, I find myself hoping this is true.

(June 22, 1999)

On the Road Without Ever
Leaving Home

I had hunted the great white whale and photographed African elephants by the time I was 13.

I rode a camel across burning Sahara sands with a caravan of silk merchants when I was only 16, and fought off fierce Bedouin raiders and beautiful belly dancers every step of the way.

I was a mercenary in the Spanish Civil War and a blockade runner in the American Civil War at age 18.

By the time I was 20, I was as familiar with Scotland's Highlands as I was with Monte Sano, and years later, while visiting friends in Ulster, the Glens of Antrim in Northern Ireland looked like they did the first time I came across them.

In the decade of my 20s, I climbed Everest with Hilary, parachuted into the jungles of Brazil hoping to locate escaped Nazis, and commanded a submarine stealing northward under the polar ice pack on a secret mission.

I was as a fly on the wall in that morose

dwelling high in Austria's Alps where Hitler and his henchmen planned war on Europe. Later, I was one of the first soldiers to arrive at Auschwitz and see the terrible sight. In fact, I was with the Jews who fled Treblinka, managing to dodge the gunfire of the guards and make it safely to the woods.

I solved murder cases with Hercule Poirot and Agatha Christie before I was 30, which excited me so much I began to tag along with Holmes and Dr. Watson, although Sherlock's personal habits were a constant discomfort to both the good doctor and me.

I have been shot at by assassins, been tricked by the most beautiful women on Earth and been allowed to read files so secret they were kept under lock and key.

I've landed in every major airport, slept in every major capital, met most every major figure who ever lived.

I've huffed and puffed with a little engine going up a hill, shed tears of happiness and sorrow in a little house on the prairie, saved a little rabbit that was starving to death.

I've ridden a fast pony across the plains with Indians, charged up a hill at Gettysburg toward the Yankees with Pickett, defended the same hill against the Rebels with Chamberlain.

I did most of these things before I was 50. But that hasn't been nearly enough. At the moment, I'm trying to solve a case about a murdered politician so I can get on to helping Emerson polish up his essays.

How have I managed to live such a life, and what did it cost? The answer's easy. I lived it through my imagination, and it only cost the price of the books.

When I visit elementary schools these days and see students in the Reading Is Fun program, I can't help but look at all of those innocent faces and feel happy for them.

Because of the simple gift of being able to read, they'll be able to go to exotic places and have exciting adventures. Because of their imaginations, they'll be able to hear, smell, taste and feel life when they want without ever leaving home. It almost makes me want to start all over again with them.

Just call me Ishmael.

(March 9, 1995)

Are We As Hopeless As This?

Rob Wheat wants to be a sportswriter after graduating from the University of Kansas.

But there are fewer newspaper sportswriting jobs available now than anytime I can remember. There aren't many jobs in several professions right now, as a matter of fact.

Rob interned at *The Times* last year, and we all have passed along job possibilities and have told him to hold his head high.

Recent college graduates and soon-to-be graduates have heard lots of that, but it still beats hearing nothing.

Rob's young and his hopes haven't had time to be dashed, so in his energetic, youthful enthusiasm he sought advice from one of his favorite sportswriters, Tom Boswell, of the *Washington Post.*

Boswell is considered by his peers to be America's top authority on the game of baseball, a designation which once offered Chicago columnist Mike Royko an opportunity to compare that with being "the tallest midget in the circus."

Royko was closer to the truth with his laughing one-liner than maybe he imagined.

Boswell answered Rob Wheat's letter by telling

him that he (Boswell) isn't a guidance counselor, newspapers are dying (which Rob said was spelled "dieing"), and Rob probably can't write, anyway.

That's how the big-time, top-ranked sportswriter encouraged the starry-eyed, nothing-kid from the Midwest.

Oh, Boswell did say, "now go and prove me wrong."

(Which I hope happens and they let me do the screenplay so I can write in a midget to play Boswell's part -- but a tall midget.)

Have we become a nation of such hopelessness that we can't offer hope to our young?

If a fancy-schmancy writer of baseball games, for Christ's sake, can use words, correctly spelled or not, to discourage a kid who only wanted a gentle pat, then we must be headed to hell in a basket.

I told Rob Wheat not to ever write any of those guys again, but to write me.

I'll do what we did in the office Monday: pass along job opportunities advertised in trade publications.

More than that, I'll give that verbal pat on the back and feed him such a diet of positive comments he'll be ready to jump across the Grand Canyon when he hangs up the phone.

Who said anything about anybody having to be a guidance counselor before they can offer other people hope?

It seems to me simple common decency is all the license needed to pour a little positive on a negative situation.

When I was a cub reporter who had those same stars in my eyes Rob Wheat now has in his, I, too, badgered my sportswriting heroes.

All of them, from Benny Marshall in Birmingham to Furman Bisher in Atlanta, heard my youthful cries and fed me with wisdom and compassion.

They didn't ignore me, and they surely didn't answer my plea with any devastating response.

All of them made honest, thoughful suggestions about how to better learn my craft and told me about mistakes they had made as they groped their way forward so that perhaps I could avoid the same pitfalls.

Of course, people were different then, and the country was, too, and we all seemed to care as much about each other as we did about ourselves.

These days, self always seems to come before others, even in matters of fragile delicacy. But I say you don't deliberately break somebody's heart and dash their hopes, even if you have to lie.

(March 31, 1992)

In a Chalet on a Hilltop
In Tennessee

GATLINBURG, Tenn. -- It's just-dark Thursday and the humps of tall mountains are outlined against a clear October night.

Light breezes rustling leaves in trees opposite our wooden deck make comforting sounds.

Thoughts of being an old-timey mountain man alone in a pristine wilderness come to mind.

Then people in the chalet down the hill start shooting fireworks. Solitude is destroyed by the loud hiss of sparklers scratching bright cuts on the sky's face. So much for paradise.

I never set foot in this Smoky Mountain tourist trap until Thursday afternoon. In all the years I worked as a sportswriter, not once did I ever drive up Highway 441 from Knoxville to look at this little burg on Pigeon Creek. Back in those days, Dolly's last name was Parton, not "wood."

Lots of people from Huntsville and places around it come here every other year, I'm told, to watch leaves change and Alabama play Tennessee in football.

They like to stay in chalets perched on mountainsides in this alpine village a short drive from Cumberland Avenue on the campus of the University of Tennessee.

The reason I came this year is some young couples talked us into it last December. Stay in a chalet from Thursday until Sunday. Ride a chartered bus to Neyland Stadium and back for the game Saturday.

Having made a living writing about sports for 15 years, being there in person doesn't mean that much to me. It was, in fact, a sacrifice. Not only was Tide against Vols on television Saturday, so was Auburn versus Florida in another game I'd like to see.

But the young folks -- Joe and Eliza Spearman, Joe and Martha Sutton, Gary and Julie Anglin, Tom and Tippi Lawson and Tom's brother Jim Lawson -- persuaded me and Pat Burruss to "chaperone" this trip.

What wasn't clear is who intended to watch the watchdogs.

This was written late Friday afternoon after clouds gathered and mountains wore shrouds of gray.

So I didn't know how the game ended, but I did know leaves here didn't look any more colorful than they did in my yard when we left Thursday.

Maybe fall's late all over the South. Maybe we got here too early. Whatever, and despite the fact two jillion other tourists in town couldn't possibly be wrong, I couldn't see what the big deal was all

214

about.

I'll have to be fair and admit my initial experience in this place dependent on income from, as Snuffy Smith would say, flatland touristers was dampened not from a light mist Friday but by the attitude of a few workers in shops and restaurants.

As experienced as I like to feel I am, I really didn't know how bad some people can dislike you if they think you're for a football team other than theirs.

I really could care less about outcomes of football games, but I can get insulted at home for lots less money.

The company, though, was top drawer. However, a large gulf separates being 50 and being 30. I had forgotten young people like to stay up late and get up early.

But I thank them for planning this last December and making me part of it.

There's something special about building memories with new friends on a cool October night in the Smokies while logs burn brightly in a fireplace.

(October 18, 1992)

Yo, 'Ratio, What It Be, My Man?

We should all apologize for what has happened and is happening to the American language.

Professional writers and commentators are as guilty as laymen, perhaps guiltier because they should know better.

A lot of what's wrong with American English is our fascination with more.

Even families who can't afford them have more than one automobile because it's the American way.

And what household would be caught dead with only one telephone and television set?

Here's how such attitudes helped change the language:

Hollywood actors considered the biggest box office draws were called stars, which set them far apart from the rest of the crowd, which was always referred to as "the respected character actor."

Somewhere along the way, simply being a star wasn't good enough, so the nation, aided and abetted, or perhaps totally influenced, by writers and commentators, decided it needed "superstars."

By this time, great had already replaced good in

describing talented athletes, painters, singers, mechanics and etceteras, so it was natural to place these "great" ones in the "superstar" category.

Does that mean the person who was a star in the old days would only be a respected character actor today? No. But excess is the United States' middle name and we'd rather have our great superstars than our good stars, even though they both are the same.

Yo, baby, they are.

Laxity in language should be expected from a society that believes "ain't" should be made an acceptable word, according to opinion polls.

Ain't as dialect in writing a story or in telling a joke is fine, but as a bonafide member of the family of words, it ain't acceptable.

As they leave the stadium, people prefer to say "Ain't gonna win 'cause we ain't got no superstars" rather than "We can't win because we don't have any stars (or good players)."

Yo, baby, it's true.

The influence of actors and singers whose careers are based on speaking and singing in slang will further erode American English as today's young people grow older.

The most-impressionable of today's youngsters are reaching adulthood believing mumbling sentences in a rap cadence is the correct way to speak.

Yo, baby, they are.

Of course, this can also be shown in a positive light regarding the young who will inherit this nation.

Once all oldtimers are dead and gone, those who've grown up in the "Yo, baby" generation can speak their own language without being corrected.

They'll no doubt want to translate all literature into a "modern" language they can understand.

They might perceive Shakespeare intended for Hamlet's death speech to go like this:

"Yo, 'Ratio, what it be, my man? Gimme five, baby. Cat done poisoned me and I ain't gonna hear no news from England."

Fortunately, or hopefully, those who don't particularly care to be around when that happens won't, and maybe those who still are can find some of Ham's poison.

Meanwhile, I hope to elude as long as possible the trap many of my colleagues have fallen into. I will try, hopefully very hard, not to make superstars out of people who would be just as happy simply being stars.

Yo, baby, I will.

(September 20, 1992)

Tuesday Was a Heavenly
Going-Home Kind of Day

ROSA -- Steady winter rains here in Blount County have turned the Locust Fork of the Warrior River into a regular little beast.

The current's running so fast and furious, rocks usually seen in the stream from the highway are hidden by the spray of rushing water skidding over and around them with the ferocity of race cars sliding through turns on a dirt track.

Kayak and canoe enthusiasts will return to a spot on this usually docile branch halfway between Blountsville and Cleveland later this year to renew friendly competition.

Locust Fork won't be so insubordinate then, however, for the so-called rainy season will be over and Mother Earth will have dried herself off with a big fluffy towel made of bright sunshine and green leaves.

Although there'll be a current strong enough to provide plenty of thrills, boaters won't have trouble spotting the tops of those rocks now hidden in the middle of the stream.

Only the very careless will be in danger of courting disaster when racing begins.

Tuesday was a bride-and-groom kind of day here where the Cumberland Plateau begins a resolute march toward Tennessee.

The sky was cloudless and blue. The temperature rose to near 70. A soft, steady wind provided the kind of humidity Southerners wish they had all year.

Someone spied a hawk flying overhead and another said that was a sign of blessing.

The day itself was almost all the blessing anyone needed, for there hadn't been one like it since maybe early last fall.

Three elderly gentlemen were taking advantage of the weather by lounging in front of the hardware store in Cleveland. Two were sitting on the sidewalk while the other was astride one of the big red Snapper mowers lined up for show outside the store. They watched solemnly as the hearse from Huntsville passed.

As far as graveyards go, the cemetery at Dailey's Chapel Methodist Church is fairly new. There are no old-style tombstones rising high into the sky with angels or crosses atop them, just modest-sized granite or marble markers with lots of 1980s or '90s death dates chiseled on their faces.

The view is pastoral: a foreground framed by a large oak tree, a background dominated by a field at the foot of a chain of small, wooded hills. The field has been plowed and planting will soon begin;

corn will probably grow there this fall.

By then the two golden-haired girls who're running across the green grass of the cemetery in wine-colored dresses with their cousins will be almost a year older.

Watching them, I wondered what they'll remember about being in that cemetery Tuesday when it's autumn and corn's growing in the field at the foot of the hills near the new grave belonging to their father.

He was born just a couple of miles from where his two young daughters were playing.

He came home for the last time on a heavenly day, and now he's part of the soil and the hills from which he sprang.

(February 26, 1998)

He Who Says It's "Cool"
Is a Fool

This column's for teen-agers, and not for people with weak stomachs.

Lay all the cigarettes I smoked end-to-end and they'd stretch from The Huntsville Times to Maple Hill. As the car drives, that's about three miles. Whether you happen to be coming or going, two hospitals are along the way.

If you're not familiar with town, Maple Hill is a cemetery and the hospitals are Huntsville and Medical Center.

Had I kept smoking, two things might have happened: (1) I might have ended up in one of those hospitals under an oxygen tent; (2) after coughing my lungs out and spitting up blood all over their white sheets for awhile, I might have died and been buried at Maple Hill.

The death certificate might have noted my demise was caused by either "lung cancer" or "emphysema," but the real reason would have been "stupidity." When I was 19, I played on two men's basketball teams in the winter and on two softball teams in the summer. I ran up and down basketball courts without breathing hard, and sometimes stayed after league games to play three-on-three until they closed the gym. I didn't smoke when I was 19.

My father did. Three-plus packs of unfiltered weeds a day. I would hear him coughing up a storm in his bed at night and wonder why he didn't quit.

But a dumb thing happened when I turned 20. I began smoking and drinking. Worse, I used that most stupid of all reasons to justify my new-found vices.

Let me tell it straight: "Peer pressure" is a pointless, foolish and profitless crutch. The words weren't invented just for you teen-agers today. It was around in my time, my father's time, his father's time and probably for all time.

When I became 20 I was a "man," and my new-found friends smoked cigarettes and drank sour-mash whiskey. Except, and I didn't notice this until later, we all smoked filter-tipped cigarettes and cut our whiskey with Coke. We apparently weren't nearly the men we thought we were.

When I was 25, a doctor told me I'd ruin my respiratory system if I didn't give up smoking. This was after I got up one morning and my bronchial tubes were so clogged I thought I'd suffocate. But, Shazam! He sprayed something down my throat and into my lungs which cleared them out so well I saluted him by lighting up as soon as I left his office.

Twenty-three years later, as it felt like somebody was standing on my chest each morning when I awoke, as I grew tired of coughing up and spitting out all the crud that collected in my lungs overnight, and as I often fought the urge to vomit in my breakfast plate, I quit smoking.

But you don't just "quit smoking" that easy. Not if you're addicted to nicotine. You must first convince your brain, who is, I assure you, a hard one to convince.

You cry and pray and go through literal hell. You fail while trying, several times. That makes you ashamed of being held captive by something you can't control. Your self-esteem plunges. You cry and pray and try again.

I smoked for 30 years. During that time I went to several funerals of friends who died of either lung cancer or emphysema, and as soon as the preacher said the last "amen" I fired one up. That kind of decision-making borders on the pathetic.

I wasted lots of my body and piles of my money smoking damned cigarettes, and I know from experience that those who tell you smoking is a cool thing to do are fools.

(February 25, 1994)

224

Symphony Didn't Need Any Help

People occasionally get concerned abut my couth, and the dear souls graciously offer a helping hand. They want to polish off the rough edges, as it were, although my closest associates maintain they might as well try to squeeze blood from a turnip.

Well, my associates are wrong. True, I feel more comfortable in jeans and sweat shirts, but I can also wear a tux with the best of 'em. And I know which one's used for what when there's more than one fork beside the plate. In other words, I'm not just another pretty face in the crowd.

Anyway, I attended a Huntsville Symphony Orchestra performance for the first time ever last Saturday night, and I'd like to say I'm mighty proud I was invited. Although I don't know an arpeggio from an amaretto, I know good stuff when I hear it, so let me say right up front what I heard the other night sounded pretty darned good to me. I mean, it was obvious this wasn't amateur night at a local bar and grill.

While I listened, it occurred to me that in the field of arts Huntsville's talent base can best be described as a veritable plethora,which means lots. A short distance from us in the Playhouse other Huntsvillians were enjoying a production put on by locals which I understand was a big hit.

We all should be proud of the level of excellence our musical and theatrical friends and neighbors have attained. Naturally, I'm no seasoned critic, but I do, as I said, know what I like. Being a novice, however, a few things did bother me. One was, the symphony audience didn't clap for a single number until intermission.

I understand this is the way it's done, but I've got to tell you the symphony's rendition of the national anthem was the best I've heard since Marvin Gaye's version at the NBA All-Star game, and I had a hard time not cheering. Another negative to me was, I saw a couple of young fellows in jeans and cardigan sweaters. Hey, this stuff's not Hank Jr. You might have expected me to show up like that, but not people in the know.

Finally, I didn't think the guest artist treated the patrons with much respect. He was up there about 20 minutes. I don't know what his take was, but I looked at the admission price on my ticket stub and felt like he owed the crowd at least one encore. He played the violin. He wasn't Charlie Daniels, but I thought he did pretty good. I guess he needed to catch the last plane out of town back to New York.

To be honest, the symphony sounded grand by

itself and didn't appear to be in need of outside agencies to influence the audience. But for what it's worth, I know a couple of local fiddle players they could get for a song next time. And encores won't be a problem because they'll have to be dragged off the stage. But it was a lovely evening, and I was amazed to notice in the program two charter HSO members still perform. They are Patricia Lundquist, who plays viola, and William A. Kates Jr., who plays tympani. And this is HSO's 30th year. Because I wanted to get the most out of the experience, I even read the critic's review in Monday's paper.

Of course, I didn't understand a word he said, but maybe if I go another time or two things will be clearer. At any rate, after listening to the orchestra and reading the review, I did feel polished and cultured enough to attempt to pass my feelings on to you. But for now, let me close with two words I wanted to shout Saturday night: Bravo! Encore!

(March 21, 1990)

VIII. Inspirations

For Those Who Live in Silence

I can hear what I want to hear.
Hounds chasing coons on a cold November night.
Waves from the Mexican gulf tumbling onto white sandy Alabama beaches.
My mother's soft voice calling me to supper.
My father's stern orders to clean my room.
Crickets in a woodpile.
Sirens on a city street at midnight.
Loud music from a jukebox.
Bear Bryant and Shug Jordan talking to their teams.
The cries of my babies late at night.
Television news.
Airplanes overhead.
Car horns.
High school bands.
Symphony orchestras.
Bluegrass bands.

Bums begging quarters.
Rain on a roof.
Wind in the trees.
The way snow crunches under a shoe.
Sons and daughters crying at funerals.
New husbands and wives laughing at weddings.
Foghorns at midnight.
The crash of trees toppled by the wind.
Pine logs crackling in a fireplace.
Guns.
Drums.
Fiddles.
Guitars.
Chainsaws chewing trees.
Traffic in the city.
Trains on rickety tracks.
Children yelling in a park.
Baseballs meeting bats.
I can hear what I want to hear, but some people can't.
Beethoven wrote Symphony No. 9 when he was totally deaf.
Part of it was ""Ode to Joy."
Schiller wrote that.
Beethoven put it to music.
And only heard it in his mind.
Imagine a musician who can not hear, but who has so much genius he doesn't need to.
I couldn't write without ears.

But then I'm not a genius.

Yet there are those who live each day without being able to hear a single word.

And they function.

How?

Imagine driving a car without being able to hear.

But they can dance by feeling the beat of the rhythm, which most of us with good hearing never feel.

I can hear and I take it for granted.

But.

If I couldn't hear music on my radio.

If I couldn't hear the Gulf of Mexico washing up on sand on a starry, starry night.

If I couldn't hear the hum of a newsroom in those hectic minutes before deadline.

And if I couldn't hear that sound that sounds like a train when the button's pushed and the press is started.

What a sad, sad life that would be.

I can hear what I want to hear.

Lightning crackling through the sky.

Bacon sizzling in a skillet.

Jet engines.

Balls being hit by golf clubs.

Waiters and waitresses yelling out orders.

Thunder.

Silence.

I can hear. I can answer when somebody

walks up behind and asks a question. I can yell and scream and curse and the sounds echo in my ears.

Who is handicapped?

Me who can listen to a voice on the other end of a phone, and then can put syllables together that the other voice can hear?

Or Beethoven, who hurried to put it all to music which he could hear before it was all gone from him?

I can hear what I want to hear, and tune it out if it gets too loud, or ignore it completely.

But what if it was taken from me and all I had left were the sounds in my head?

(March 6, 1991)

Chessie Saw the Orphans
As a Gift From God

Chessie Harris did what most only pretend to do: She trusted God. God didn't disappoint her, either. And she never disappointed Him.

Since her death watch began, my most recurring recollection of this remarkable woman was her rock-solid faith.

"It'll happen when it's time," she told family and friends recently. The time came Monday morning, after 91 wonderfully productive years.

Officially, she was Mrs. George Harris, but everybody simply called her Chessie.

"She (or he) was one of Chessie's children," they'd say. Or "Go see Chessie; she'll take care of you."

I tried to call her Mrs. Harris when we first met. She smiled a big, toothy smile and said, "Just call me Chessie, 'cause I'm just gonna call you Bill."

No one knows how many abandoned children or desperate mothers she ministered to as the guardian angel of the downtrodden and the down-and-out.

Numbers aren't important, though. What's important is the role she played and the void she filled simply because she felt it was her duty. Well, she felt it was more of a directive than a duty.

"I have no choice," she said to me once. "God chose me to do this. And I will."

What He chose her to do was start the Harris Home for Children with her late husband, George, where hundreds of black boys and girls, from infants to teens, lived and learned - and then longed to return to well after they were grown and gone.

After "retiring" as the home's director, she led a program that provided food and necessities for single mothers whose children would have had to do without otherwise.

The commodity she provided the most of was love.

Ask anyone who lived there what they got most from the Harris Home and they'll say love. Chessie had an abundance of it in her large heart.

"I just can't stand to think about a poor little child out there on the streets alone at night with no place to go," she said the first time I met her.

She said she asked God what to do about those children. He said to take care of them. She said it had to be the right thing to do because "we're all orphans."

To those who often wondered how she thought she could take care of so many children, she simply replied, "God will provide."

She believed it, too, and the proof of His provision has been heard in all the prayers sent to heaven on her behalf during her illness by men and women who found sanctuary in the Harris Home when they were only children.

Chessie will be celebrated in headlines as one who devoted her adult life to helping others.

The headlines will be correct, but they won't tell the whole story.

Maybe it can't be told, for that story is essentially known only to the two: Chessie and God.

But I'm certain of this:

Chessie Harris was maybe the most dedicated, determined person I ever met, and my belief in the goodness of humanity was elevated by knowing her.

(June 10, 1997)

Not Ready for the Obit Column Yet

The first things you notice about Clinton Parker is that he has a brown right eye and a blue left one.

"Wasn't born that way," says he, a slow grin spreading beneath his gray mustache.

"Had some trouble with the left one and I guess it turned that way." Seated on a chair in front of a television set, the old black man surveys his cluttered domain.

Parker's Shoe Hospital has been a Huntsville institution since 1947. A framed resolution on a wall from the Madison County Commission proclaims its owner to be a "Trail Blazer Entrepreneur" from the Minority Economic Summit and Minority Business Exposition of 1989. Clinton Parker is the last black city businessman from this era.

He wanted to be a dentist "because I liked to make teeth." But after the army and graduation from Alabama A&M with degrees in tailoring and shoe repair, he chose the life of a cobbler.

"Wasn't no money in tailoring," he explains.

All these years later, he still practices his

trade on that little block of Meridian Street not re-routed by I-565 construction.

Meridian's new path hurt him some. "People don't look as hard for you anymore," he says. Plus, they can leave shoes at repair places in big malls "and go shopping while their shoes are being fixed." But at age 75, he continues on with a very good reason for why he won't quit.

"I ain't got no hobby," he says, eyes twinkling behind horn-rimmed glasses, "and if I didn't do this, next thing I know I'd be in the obituary column. Every morning when I get up , I need an objective, I need the money, but I could do without it. I just want to be down here because it gives me something to look forward to."

He says he was feeling bad Monday night "but when I got down here Tuesday morning I started feeling good."

Last week, Clinton Parker made $33 repairing shoes. "I ain't never made that little in any week." "But," he says quickly, "The Lord will give you what you sincerely ask for." And this is a sincere man who quotes scripture and says "it bothers me" to be the last of the old businessmen "because there should be more black people in business."

But he's proud of the fact he can stay open because of customers cultivated over the years and because of the First Baptist Church congregation of which he is a member.

236

He watches news on television, but pays little attention to the rest of it because "most of the stuff you look at now you'd be better off not knowing it. It's some man taking another man's wife or killing somebody."

Clinton Parker is a philosopher. "You do a good job at home with your kids and it'll show up there," he says, pointing out the window, "because it ain't nothing in the street but trouble. I always told mine the way to be a nothing is to do nothing."

He also has all of his equipment paid for because "you pay for what you buy as you go along and you won't never be in no trouble." So it doesn't bother him when he has a $33 week. His attitude is, "Trouble helps a person grow stronger. I'm happy doing this, and that's where you need to be."

(September 19, 1990)

If I Could Be As Free As Kenny

Kenny mentioned two reasons why he likes living in the Old Town historic district.

"I can walk to every place where I have to pay my bills," and, "It's nice being where there are trees and seeing squirrels play."

Major streets like Jordan Lane and Memorial Parkway were between him and where he paid bills when he lived on the west side of town, meaning he too often depended on the generosity of others to drive him downtown.

"There sure weren't any squirrels where I lived, and there were hardly any trees," he said.

Now his apartment near Five Points "is just perfect," and California Street's the only big traffic artery he has to contend with.

But he knows the times of day when traffic's light, plus he can always go a couple of blocks to Clinton Avenue and cross at a traffic light.

Being able to go to Huntsville Utilities and South Central Bell when he needs to and not when others can is exactly the way he wants it.

That's because he's as independent a person as you'll ever meet. Some say too independent, and worry about him a lot. He's sorry about being such a bother, but he's not going to change his style.

Holing up in a room and cursing his bad luck would be easy, but he'd rather travel the road least traveled.

That's why all he has to do is sit in a strange car once to be able to open and close the door and also operate the seat belt without help. He knows you mean well when you try to lend a hand. It's just that he'd rather do it himself.

Doing it himself is real important to both his confidence and his self-esteem.

The reason it's so important is he's blind.

Kenny walking briskly along with his cane tapping the sidewalk in front of him is familiar to those of us who live downtown.

The quickness of his pace and the fact he's usually alone make some folks nervous. He's blind for goodness sakes! He might get run over!

They wouldn't worry so much if they'd spend a few minutes with him. Ken can control himself. He can't control what others do, but, then, neither can folks who can see.

If he ever does get hit, I'm betting it's not his fault.

We could all learn positive lessons if we spent time with people who have attitudes like Kenny.

Instead of retreating to his dark world he did something about living where he had to depend on others.

He moved to an entirely new environment and then learned the streets so well he can now come and go as he pleases.

A family lives above him and a friend lives across the hall from him, and they're there on those occasions when he does need help.

Mostly, though, he goes it alone with his trusty cane, and maybe somebody's elbow to lightly touch now and then when negotiating tight turns he has never seen.

Yes, "seen," and I meant to use the word, because in his own way he sees just as clearly as if nothing was wrong with his eyes. If you can describe the scene, he can see it in his mind. That's how he's able to talk about trees and squirrels now that he lives in a place where they are.

If I, with my two good eyes, could see half as well as Kenny sees, how joyous my heart would be, and how free my soul would feel.

(October 11, 1992)

The Passing of a Special Kind of Girl

She had open-heart surgery when she was 6 hours old.

"Don't worry about this baby," a nurse told one of the grandmothers. "She's got a bad temper - and she's gonna survive."

Lilie Hill Knapp wasn't special because she lived through her heart being operated on twice. She was special because her personality was as relentless as a magnet. People clung to her on her short journey through life.

The girl they called Hill died last Thursday, a week after suffering a heart attack on maybe her most important night.

Because her late paternal grandparents, C. David and Myrtie Knapp, had wished it, she was presented at the annual Beaux Arts Krewe Ball in their hometown, Birmingham, where Hill was born.

Swept along by warm applause, she had just made her way around the auditorium when her heart quit on the night of Feb. 7.

Medical personnel tried hard, but couldn't

save her. She was only 20.

A host of friends descended on the hospital where Hill lay in a coma. Only it was a life watch, not a death watch, for they stood at her bed and told her the latest jokes, or simply talked.

They felt she could hear, so they urged her, begged her, to open her eyes and come back to them.

One girl who graduated with Hill from Huntsville High School quit her job in Kentucky to come be with her stricken friend. Her employer wouldn't let her have time off. "But I have to be there," she said.

The family met at the home of Mr. and Mrs. Thornton Fleming, Hill's maternal grandparents, after Monday's funeral to talk about what the support of those young people meant.

All agreed the caring and compassion demonstrated by Hill's friends proved, as one said, "There are still as many good young people out there who will give you support and devotion" as there are bad ones who won't.

As much as she'll be missed by her parents, Roberta Spragins Hill and David Knapp, her brothers will probably miss her most of all.

She was the middle child between Forrest, 23, and Hayes, 18. Forrest said she was "the purest, sweetest girl I know, and there's not many like that these days. She was a great friend of mine, if nothing else."

Hayes said, "I'll miss talking to her every night - and seeing her act goofy."

Their sister, who was a child development major at Alabama, wanted to be a hospital therapist for pre-schoolers.

She made that decision when she was 9, after her second open-heart operation. She had been inspired by a therapist named Laura, whose compassion made what turned out to be a lasting impression on Hill. And in the end, Hill's death has caused many who knew her to reach out to loved ones they've been needing to reach out to.

(February 18, 1997)

It Won't Rain on God's Child

This is a fable.

Athletes from the city and county school systems are gathered for a big track meet. A band's playing, flags are flying and excitement's out of control. Field events are being held at each end of the stadium, and races are being run one after another on the track.

Except for words printed on handmade banners, no individual school affiliations are displayed. The athletes are dressed alike, white T-shirts with blue insignia. Fans not only are cheering their favorites, they're raising a ruckus for everybody else.

And get this. No scores are being kept, so no school can claim it won. Not only that, everybody competing gets a ribbon. When the athletes go to the awards stand to receive ribbons, all the others pat them on the back, hug their necks, and yell as wildly as if they'd won. It is, in fact, a track meet without school-versus-school or city versus-county rivalry.

It's being conducted the way you only dream of a big athletic event featuring neighboring high schools to be conducted in an atmosphere of good will and harmony.

A fable. Except it happened Thursday. The annual Huntsville-Madison County Special Olympics at Milton Frank Stadium is the only "pure" sporting event you'll ever see. Pure because competitors don't run and jump and throw in order to attract attention of college scouts.

They don't let leg cramps, thigh bruises, or sore big toes keep them out of the lineup. And when they cross the finish line sixth in a field of six, they still punch holes in the sky with their fists and leap on somebody, anybody's, back.

They don't run and jump and throw for the glory, they do it for the sheer exuberance and the unbridled joy just being part of it's produces.

Listen, Coach, next time one of your star players can't play because of a head cold, tell him or her about the 5-year-old fellow with Downs Syndrome who has also had open heart surgery and won a blue first place ribbon in a foot race Thursday.

Tell him or her about the little blind girl who ran her race holding to a rope they stretched down the track. Better yet, bring your team to the Special Olympics, sit 'em in the stands, then tell 'em to pay attention.

Make 'em see how the other athletes don't have to be told to go congratulate winners. Tell "em to watch how everybody cheers for everybody else. Then tell "em this happens because all these athletes love and respect and care for one another.

You can also tell yours that those athletes train weeks for just this one event, and that it'll be a whole year before they'll get to compete in front of a crowd again, and that a simple, colored ribbon pinned on their chests mean as much to them as any state championship statue in your school's trophy case.

Then you might as well tell "em it's very possible one or two of those boys and girls limping down the track or racing in their wheelchairs won't be around to be a Special Olympian next year. If you do all that, I'll bet your next practice would be the best one you've ever had.

You notice it didn't rain until Thursday afternoon, after the games were over. The local Special Olympics has never been rained out. One regional official explained why.

"It won't rain on God's children," she said.

(April 19, 1991)

Safe By His Mother's Side
at the End

The week he died, Erik Tillery told his family he wanted to go back to school at Auburn as soon as he was better. Those around him saw how weak he was and knew the pain he lived with shrugged their shoulders and nodded knowingly. Why not. It was typical of his attitude.

Erik was only 19 when he died on the afternoon of April 8. It wasn't leukemia that killed him. It was respiratory problems he developed from a bone marrow transplant six years ago.

In an age with positive role models are as scarce as hen's teeth, Eric Tillery was as refreshing as a warm Gulf breeze on a soft Southern night. In his motorized chair, and with his quick and dry since of humor, he inspired his classmates at Lee High School for the short time he was among them. For a fact, he graduated in the top 12 in his class. And on the day diplomas were presented in the Spring of 1991, Lee's seniors stood and cheered when he rolled across the stage to get his piece of paper.

Lee Principal Tom Owen, a former football coach and no stranger to acts above and beyond the call said this: "He was a tremendously courageous young man, He was bright, and he always had a smile. He was as inspiration to our kids."

Erik was diagnosed with leukemia when he was 12. His brother, Darren, was the donor for a bone marrow transplant in 1984. And although the cancer went into remission, Erik suffered other side effects from the operation. He had joint contractions in his hands, hips and legs, and thus the motorized chair. He became easy prey for pneumonia. Hardly a day passed when he wasn't in pain.

Through it all, he retained an incredible sense of humor, which, in turn, helped his mother, Gaye; his brother; his older sister, Alicia Cantrell; his younger sister, Haley, and his other family members survive the ordeal in better shape.

He never asked for special favors. "Erik was in pain most of the time, but people who visited never saw it,"said Gaye. "He would laugh and joke with them, and when they left he would break down in tears and ask for a pain pill."

Haley, a seventh-grader at Westlawn, said once when they were alone he griped about how ugly he thought he looked. She told him, "You look beautiful to me." That made him his smiling, friendly self again.

His aunt, Judy Bowers, praised Erik for his independent nature, and for the fact "he was always thankful his problems were not as bad as others." Blessed with a brilliant mind, Erik enrolled at Auburn to study physics. It was one of his goals. Another was to learn to drive.

His mother sold her car to buy the specially equipped van he used to get around campus. But he was at Auburn only three weeks last fall when he got sick and had to come home. Right up until the end, he intended to return. Near that end, Erik told his mother he was scared. She told him she was, too. It was, she said, the first time she saw him cry.

He made a little will that said he didn't want to be kept alive by a respirator. When it was obvious death was near, Erik called his mother to his side and said, "I gotta tell you, there couldn't have been a better mother. "Gaye replied, "There couldn't have been a better son."

Erik had been comatose for about two days on the day he died. Gaye said as she watched him, she was moved to lie in his bed and put her arm around him. In about three minutes, he quietly passed. It was almost as if he had been waiting for her to hold him in her arms one last time.

(April 18, 1990)

Of Goodness and a Man Recovering His Dignity

It was only 8 o'clock Saturday morning, but Fred Baldwin was busy showing off.

He sped down a hall, popped his version of a "wheelie" and stopped on a dime. Then he backed up, spun around and took off again.

The smile on his face looked like the grille of a Buick Roadmaster. Although he had only had it for less than 24 hours, workers at the home where he lives said the new wheelchair had already made Fred a different man.

The old one he used was outdated at worst and cumbersome at best. Fred kind of lumbered around like a turtle trying to cross a busy highway when he used it. Because it had lost some of its essential parts, he also had to be strapped in like a baby in a highchair to keep from slumping over.

Cerebral palsy is bad enough without having to live like that. The problem was his old wheelchair was beyond repair and a new one would cost about $11,000.

Fred's family couldn't afford that kind of

money and the agency that takes care of him didn't have that kind of discretionary money. Practically grounded because of his plight, Fred had begun to spend more time in his room watching television and less time going on those field trips he loves so much.

A naturally outgoing person who basically never meets a stranger, Fred had become withdrawn and, a staff member noted, "had gotten depressed."

That was the situation several months ago when Fred was the subject of a Saturday feature in The Huntsville Times.

Today's story is more about goodness than it is about a new wheelchair, for Fred would still be bumbling around in that old thing if some people hadn't had generous hearts.

Some of those who read about Fred's plight began to send money to the Volunteers of America (VOA), the agency in charge of the residence where Fred lives.

Folks on fixed incomes sent $10 checks with notes that said "this is not much, but I hope it helps."

Ten dollars here, 20 dollars there. Most of it was sent by people who know what it means to struggle from one paycheck to another. But they were all bound together by the common bond of decency.

Then, like a miracle, two prominent Huntsville citizens, a lawyer and a businessman, each made very generous contributions to Fred's wheelchair fund.

The rest, as they say, is ecstasy. Well, at any rate Fred is ecstatic. His outlook has been lifted from the dungeons of despair and his attitude and self-esteem have changed radically.

How does he like his brand, spanking new "Quickie P200" with its leather head rest and seat and the handy control switch?

"All right!" he said, trademark megawatt smile plastered across his face.

Just to make sure those reading this understand exactly how he feels, Fred Baldwin asked me to say he always remembers to thank God every night for his blessings - and for all those people who bought him his new wheelchair.

(August 2, 1998)

His Legacy of Belief Is Lasting

Great men aren't always those whose biographies are best known. It's not necessary for their names to be on everyone's lips. They often distinguish themselves while working in relative obscurity.

All great men have one thing in common: good deeds that live long after their bodies die.

Such a man was Rev. George J. Wheeler, and many were they who sat through his funeral Friday at Murphy Hill Baptist Church whose memories centered on personal contact with this genuine man of God.

Like most newspaper death notices, his skipped over his life like flat rocks skip over the surface of water. It told his age, named survivors, said he was a war veteran and mentioned his college education. It didn't reveal much concerning the essence of the man.

One sentence in the obituary about how he "pastored three churches in Huntsville" did come close to telling who he was. Those Baptist churches were East Huntsville, Oak Park and Twickenham. The Rev. Wheeler helped start all three.

I don't know how others at the funeral remembered him, but to me George Wheeler was a healer of broken hearts and a fixer of shattered dreams. That's because he was one of God's men. But since he conducted himself with true humility and lived in biblical dignity, only those he affected knew it.

Lucky for me I was one of those whose life was influenced by this quiet but powerful preacher of the Good News.

I met him more than 30 years ago when a screw in my rudder worked loose and I was drifting on seas of doubt and insecurity. He waded out into the waters, as it were, and pulled me ashore. Then we became friends.

I was sports editor of The Times. He was an older fellow insistent on dating himself by calling me "Grantland," as in Grantland Rice, a New York sports writer of olden days. Rice was one of my heroes, so I didn't mind. But I called him "preacher" or "Reverend Wheeler," for even though he wouldn't have cared, "George" would have been too disrespectful in my mind.

When we'd meet anywhere years later, "There's Grantland" he'd say, and "Hello, Preacher," I'd reply.

Many thoughts filled me when I saw him in his coffin the other evening. Photographs of his two grandsons were placed against his right hand, and I worried about how sad not having their grandfather would be for them. But when several students from the bible college where he taught gathered at his casket to pray, my mood changed and I thought about how proud of his memory those boys will be able to be.

Lolene Wheeler said a small smile was on his lips when she found him dead in bed the other night, so the passing couldn't have been bad, and those who loved him are thankful.

"He was a good man, a good husband and a good pastor," Mrs. Wheeler said. "He loved the Lord."

As one of those who preached the funeral said, Rev. George Wheeler, like Enoch, walked with God.

(December 11, 1994)

IX. Looking Around

An Event Whose
Image Is Faultless

NEW MARKET -- There's always talk about an event being "bigger and better next year." Sometimes it is. Sometimes it isn't. The Older Americans Festival is.

Tuesday in sunshine and in shade, the biggest crowd in festival history gathered under tall pines on the banks of the lake at Sharon Johnston Park to eat, drink and be merry.

Like the previous seven years, they did all three.

Over 3,000 souls from five counties participated in the biggest annual non-sporting event dinner-on-the-ground in Alabama. They came by car, truck, van, chartered bus and church bus to eat hot barbecued chicken and cold ice cream.

They came from Madison, Limestone, Jackson, Marshall and DeKalb counties to hear singers sing and see dancers dance.

Some have attended all eight festivals, but a lot showed up yesterday for the first time because friends told them how much fun they'd have.

Some there were 99 years old, but on a day with nothing but blue skies overhead and the scent of grilled chicken being carried by the wind through the trees, age was relative.

Relative to how well catfish were biting, how funny clowns were, and how good music was.

People had a good time at the country picking and fiddling stage, loved the square dance exhibition, and applauded all entertainment on the covered dock in the lake.

Tony Mason sang mixed favorites, like he does every year, Ed White Middle School's show choir took the crowd to Disney World, Hazel Green's high school choir was superb, and The Alpha Quartet reached deep for basic gospel.

The crowd listened reverently to Alpha's version of "God Bless America," then clapped time when the ensemble quickened the pace with "Have a Little Talk With Jesus."

That one even had people leaning against tree trunks, tapping their toes.

The Older Americans Festival, sponsored by the Top of Alabama Regional Council of Governments (TARCOG) Area Agency on Aging and the Madison County Commission, was intended to be sort of a picnic in the beginning.

There was a fairly large crowd the first year,

and everybody involved said, well, that's good, we'll have it again.

Next year came and it got bigger, then bigger, until yesterday when it was the biggest of all.

Lots of individuals, companies and corporations now regularly donate money as sponsors, and lots of people donate time as volunteers. It happens, though, because a core of dedicated people from TARCOG and the Madison County Commission make it happen.

It's the job of people from the Area Agency on Aging to minister to senior citizens. But this yearly picnic's well above the call of duty. These people do this because they have conviction in their hearts.

So every year about the third week in May they invite every senior citizen at the top of Alabama to their party.

And for a few hours the boredom of limited daily routines is replaced by the kind of excitement being in the company of lots of people generates. There was a multitude at Sharon Johnston Park on Tuesday, and Alpha's little talk with Jesus must have done the trick, because it was a faultless day for a picnic.

(May 20, 1992)

259

When Beauty Is
Smudged by Rascals

The trails of the Huntsville Land Trust on the lower slopes of Monte Sano offer clear evidence of nature's endurance and man's deceit. The dozen miles of hiking paths in the Land Trust preserve are a testament to the strength and beauty of the great outdoors.

Tuesday, in the high-70s heat of a false spring day, Loop Trail offered an invitation too special to ignore.

From a tall persimmon tree about to bud to a well-worn game track crossing the rocky descent where wanderers come to lose themselves in quiet beauty, the wood where Land Trust land lies next to Toll Gate Road and Bankhead Parkway was in elegant form.

The forest has forgotten the snowdrifts and icicles of only yesterday. But for a few broken branches and a large tree that fell across the trail, there were no visible scars from the rigors of winter. Fresh green moss growing by the walk and on huge gray boulders planted in the mountain's face confirmed creation believes the worst is behind us.

Bright yellow forsythia is blooming. And hepatica, the pretty white flower that always heralds spring. So, too, is lonicera fragrantissima, the "most fragrant honeysuckle" from southern China that gives the wood a faintly sweet scent in early spring.

Probably deposited here by the droppings of birds, this prolific Oriental emigrant is delightful to smell but poses a serious threat to some of the preserve's endangered plants, such as the wild flower called clematis morefieldii, which only grows in rare places, the Land Trust plot being one of them.

The Huntsville Land Trust has about 150 volunteers helping to maintain this public treasure, including Boy Scouts, the Sierra Club, participants of the Chamber of Commerce Youth Leadership Class and other assorted individuals and groups.

Under their stewardship, this sanctuary has fast become a safe harbor in the center of society's turbulent sea. Just minutes from Courthouse Square, the solitude of the place is deafening. And that makes you wonder why rascals ever have to wander by.

They built a bench, the volunteers did, and put it at a lively intersection created by several trails. There the intrepid explorer could rest tired legs and weary feet while listening to the babbling brook called Fagan Creek, which rushes down the mountain. No more tranquil setting in Madison County can be imagined.

As you probably have guessed, the bench has been torn from its moorings and stolen. An iron rod encased in cement and cast into the bushes is all that remains of the resting place.

Who stole the bench is a puzzle, and why they wanted it is an even bigger mystery, but the fact it's gone proves that some among us always will have neither an eye for beauty nor an appreciation for reverence.

They stole from themselves, for the Land Trust retreat belongs to everyone, and all of us should treat it with the same kind of respect we give to our personal property.

(February 29, 1996)

Cooking Has a Couple of Meanings in This Hollow

LYNCHBURG, Tenn. -- There was a time when smoke rising from a hollow in North Alabama or South Tennessee brought revenue agents running. But not here, where making whiskey is legal.

The Jack Daniel's Distillery is world-famous - especially this time of year when Christmas dinner is being served twice daily at Miss Mary Bobo's Boarding House.

English spoken with foreign accents can be heard all around the Moore County Courthouse Square, and tourists are here for one of three reasons:

A visit to the distillery.

A meal at Miss Bobo's.

-- Both of the above.

The gazebo was being dressed for the season on the first day of December; festive greenery shared space with red and blue Yuletide lights while two men were putting up the county's Christmas tree. "It's not so big this year," one of the workers said as several of us stopped to admire a 10-footer he and his partner had planted. "We usually have one so big we have to use a crane to set the thang up,"

263

he said with a friendly smile.

Folks in these hills and hollows are always affable, but more so this time of year, for friendliness and folksiness are part of Lynchburg's mystique.

A grocery store, a bank and two or three eating places occupy some of the buildings on the square, but the rest of the space is filled by antique and collectible shops.

For a town of less than 700 in a county of about 5,000, tourism is the straw that stirs the drink, so to speak.

In the place where the famous "Old No. 7" black label sour mash is cooked, the strongest thing you can have in your drink is the caffeine in your coffee or tea.

But you can buy plenty of Jack Daniel's paraphernalia.

From letter openers to back-yard barbecue grills to golf shirts, there's plenty of stuff to be had with the Daniel's monogram on it. However, you'll have to wait until you get to places like Huntsville or Nashville before you can sample some of Mr. Jack's sippin' whiskey. If you're lucky enough to have a reservation to the 11 a.m. or the 1 p.m. seatings at Miss Bobo's, though, you won't have to wait to sample some of the South's finest country cooking.

Dinner ("Don't call it lunch!") at Miss Bobo's is an experience to be savored any time of the year.

During December, it's a special feast.

(Psst! Some of the dishes are laced with just the tiniest trace of Old No. 7.)

Unfortunately, it might be easier to find tickets to the Masters Golf Tournament than to get a seat at Miss Bobo's dinner table this month, although they will gladly add your name to a waiting list. Meanwhile, tell-tale smoke above the trees in Jack Daniel's hollow means hickory's being burned and sour mash is being cooked, but no one's worried about "revenooers" busting up the still. From his vantage point in the cemetery on the hill above town, one wonders what the man who started it all thinks about his hollow now.

(December 4, 1997)

He Wants to Do What
He Wants to Do

ARDMORE, Tenn.-- It was high noon, and the tall, graying man with a receding hairline and wire-rimmed glasses squinted in the light cast by a dim bulb, eyed the cue ball, lined up the shot.

With a flick of his pool stick the ball rolled across the velvety green table and lightly kissed another ball, which disappeared into a side pocket.

His opponent, a young man who had stopped by to look at an antique car and play a quick game of pool, grinned at an interested observer. "He's played this game before," dead-panned the young man. It was a slow day at the 31 Blue Spot, and the tall man was just killing time.

Shooting pool in the middle of the day and selling a few cold bottles of beer from a drive-through window to locals on their lunch hours has been Robert Crabtree's lifestyle for about as long as he can remember.

But at age 77, the thrill is gone, and the man who owns maybe the most famous club in the region is ready to retire.

"As the little boy said," Crabtree explained,

"I've done what I had to do all my life, now I want to do what I want to do."

What he wants to do is spend more time with his children and play around with his walking horses.

The horses are only a hobby. The 31 Blue Spot was, and is, his life. Plus a couple of other places he owned before he bought the long, low watering hole along Highway 31 on the Tennessee side of Ardmore. Born in Petersburg, Tenn., Crabtree's family moved to Ardmore when he was 12, "and Fayetteville is the furtherest I've lived from here, except when I was in the service four years in World War II."

He owned Steve's Cafe in Fayetteville from 1966 to 1969, then bought what he named Bob's Place, which is down the highway from the Blue Spot near Interstate 65. He sold Bob's in 1977 and bought the Blue Spot in 1979.

The Blue Spot was always famous for weekend dances, but Crabtree quit hiring bands a couple of years ago "because they got to wanting too much and I couldn't afford it."

Yet it remains one of the favorite rendezvous of the club crowd or the simply thirsty, a living, breathing legend whose reputation as a fun place to be is secure.

Robert Crabtree was married three times. He has two sons, Johnny Lee and Jerry Boyd, from his first marriage to Lucille Sullivan; a daughter,

Lisa, from his second to Elizabeth Ray; and an adopted daughter, Dweese Warren, from his third to Martha Hicks.

Lucille died in a car wreck in 1956, Elizabeth died in 1957, and Martha died two years ago after she and Crabtree had been married 32 years.

Now the Blue Spot with its pure white oak floor and polished pine ceiling is on the auction block.

"I want to quit worrying," Crabtree said. "I want to get a one-shot deal with this capital gains thing. I want to get my retirement straightened out. I ain't got too much time left and I want to enjoy it."

The aging barkeep added, "I know I'm gonna miss it, but I never had a habit I couldn't quit. I quit smoking and drinking. I drank less in this business than I did before I went into it."

With that, he sounded a warning to potential buyers: "Pleasure and business don't mix, and anybody who buys a place like this and parties big time won't last."

After he sells the 31 Blue Spot? "I want to get around and see the kids. I'll stay busy messing with my hobbies. I ain't never been dissatisfied too much in my life."

(August 19, 1993)

King Cotton: Life Without His Majesty Is Woeful

The land of cotton lies lifeless on these warm September days, a sad sight for Southern eyes to see.

From Hazel Green to New Hope and from Madison to Gurley, the fields of fall stand empty, victims of too many rainy days and cool nights last spring.

The giant picking machines which changed the face of the industry sit idly in sheds while the trailers used to haul cotton to gins are lined up in rows behind barns.

The call they're waiting for won't come this year.

"It was the most devastating thing I believe I've ever seen when they told us to bush hog the cotton," said Frances Darwin, whose husband's family has been in farming since the 1800s.

Except for one year when there was an early frost, Buddy Darwin said, it's the first time he hasn't had a cotton crop to harvest since he was 18.

Darwin and his employees have stayed busy

because his farm also raises corn and soybeans and he also has a thriving popcorn business. But this has been a lonely, costly season for the farmers and ginners who concentrate on cotton.

There now are only stubs or stalks where once there was a sea of cotton for as far as the eye could see. In normal times, the rural areas of Madison County and its neighbors would be covered now with white bolls ready for the pickers. These are abnormal times, though, and the devastation reaches near and far.

The economic impact is a hard pill to swallow: a local cotton gin has been sold and will move to Tennessee, some farmers had no crop insurance, workers employed by gins and cotton farms lost jobs.

Truckers and cotton warehouses and cottonseed oil mills also suffered, and the true extent of the economic catastrophe may never be known.

Farmers are gamblers who bet against the house, and the house is controlled by Mother Nature, a formidable croupier who occasionally calls in her marks.

It rained almost every day for six weeks last spring, throwing cotton three weeks to a month behind. Experts from the Auburn Extension Service called the crop a disaster. Crop insurance companies agreed, and the 1997 harvest was plowed under.

Those few fields that weren't ground up this year are hopeless images of their former selves when cotton in the South was truly king.

The day the crop insurance people told him the king was dead, Buddy Darwin said he couldn't accompany the bush hogs to his fields because he "just couldn't bear to see them running."

Like others in the business, he was trying to save his cotton "up until the day the crop insurance folks appraised it and said destroy it."

There's always hope in a farmer's heart, though, and Darwin said he doesn't believe cotton "will ever leave North Alabama."

But considering the calamity the farm community suffered this year, Buddy Darwin also feels "folks will become more diversified in the future, and I don't think they will be as obligated to cotton."

(September 23, 1997)

A Virtuoso at the End of a Passage

GILBERT'S CROSSROADS -- His work's not on museum walls or library shelves, but George Thomas Keahey is nevertheless an artiste.

"Tommy" Keahey has lived on Sand Mountain in a house trailer beside DeKalb County Highway 43 for two years. But if his homestead took him miles from his true love, the river, the aging virtuoso kept plenty of reminders. They can't help but be noticed from the road, for they're how he got his alias.

Take a business card from Keahey and you'll find "Net Man" printed on it instead of his name. You won't find a telephone number, either, for he has no phone. To do business, you either visit or write in care of Route 1, Dawson.

"Ain't no route two," he said. It was Wednesday and about to rain. Wind blew, Sally the part-chow, part-Belgian spitz puppy barked, and a big pot of green peas and "fresh hog jaw" cooking on the stove smelled magnificent.

Several fish traps swayed in the wind on a line strung next to an old Ford truck parked by the road. Two simple signs painted on the truck hid a complex story. One said "Fisherman 37 Years," the other "53 Years of Net Making." It's 55 years now. Keahey hasn't fished since becoming unable to haul nets, but he still makes them. And making nets is what he's all about.

Not just nets, but nets with a world-class reputation, for fishermen far and wide have queued up for Net Man's artistry.

George Keahey makes them with his hands. His top- of- the- line stuff features cotton twine, tight knots and a lifetime of loving experience. He'll sell you one with a 22-inch mouth for $10, about half what you pay at stores which also buy his nets.

But, of course, you have to find Gilbert's Crossroads to get the good deal.

"I come from around Section and Macedonia and Scottsboro," Keahey said, "and I fished the Tennessee, the Warrior and the Coosa, and I done some deep sea fishing." To him, fishermen who take catfish "six inches long have just about ruined the river and all the rivers have gotten polluted so badly they've just about ruined the fish." Keahey learned net tying from Tom Phillips and Joe Hale, "two old-time fishermen from around Scottsboro," while in his teens. "I can sit down and tie up a pair of britches that'll fit you now," he said. Unfortunately, his fingers have begun to limit the number of hours he spends at his craft, and the drop in his output worries the old man.

George Keahey is 75 "and what stock I got now

is probably it." Tying one net takes over two hours of constant work, "and I just can't sit still that long no more." He can't spend as much time in his workshop because arthritis, old age and injury have caused him to have "a world of damned trouble." Neither can he get one of his 12 children, his many grandchildren nor any of his friends involved in learning the craft. "Nearly all the fishermen in the old days could tie nets," he mused, "but I don't know anybody now. And I can't get anybody interested." Hooking one thumb in a shoulder strap of his Liberty overalls, he smiled, shook his head, and gestured at the nets and traps hung from the ceiling and the walls of his workshop. "Take a look," he sadly said. "When they're gone, that's it." Then Net Man grabbed his walker and started for his trailer. Sally trotted after him. The aroma of green peas and hog jaw sailed on the blowing wind.

(March 11, 1994)

Miss Julia: A Lifetime
of Devotion and Service

News that gold was discovered in California spread eastward like a grass fire out of control in 1849.

Midwesterner Frank Gasson was one who became a "49er" by rushing west. But he felt the overland trip would be too wild for his wife, Henrietta. He sent her by ship around the horn of South America. It took her five hard months to reach him in the gold fields.

Julia Harless chuckled while telling about her grandfather and grandmother, but to prove the story's happy ending, she showed a gold ring Frank made for Henrietta after striking it rich.

Not only does "Miss Julia" have a treasure trove of family stories, she has her own fertile imagination for writing children's tales and a God-given talent for painting to draw from.

All of this helped her profess to having had "a good life" on the eve of a milestone which never crossed her mind when she was young. Tuesday afternoon at First United Methodist Church, where she sang in a choir until she was 92, and where the nursery is named in her honor for the work she did with handicapped children, Julia G. Harless will be honored on her 100th birthday.

Miss Julia was born in Delphos, Ohio, to newspaperman D.V. Gasson and Laura Sevitz Gasson, whose father, Thomas Sevitz, was the town tax collector.

She found the man who became her husband when her father went to work for the newspaper in Gadsden, Ala.

Lee D. Harless worked at Cooney's Department Store, where she was modeling diamonds when they met. They married and moved to Huntsville, where Harless worked for Dunnavant's Department Store on Washington Street from 1928 to 1960.

They had three children: Jane Harless Ward is married to a retired college professor, Dr. Robert D. Ward, and lives in Statesboro, Ga.; noted local artist Lee D. Harless Jr. is married to Carol Anderson Harless; Virginia Harless Cook is married to NASA engineer Lewis J. Cook Jr.

There are three grandchildren, two step-grandchildren and one great-grandchild for Miss Julia to love. Just last year, she wrote six short stories which were bound into a booklet for great- granddaughter Jennifer, who lives in Montana.

Although her eyesight's poor and she doesn't paint much anymore, Miss Julia feeds birds in her back yard every day and won't miss her favorite soap operas on television.

Attended by Mary Wright and Obinetta Solomon, she lives in her own house and said she's "doing fine."

While going to the moon is the most astonishing thing she's witnessed, Miss Julia said "everything" invented in her lifetime "has been remarkable to me."

She drove until one day when she was "going to Big Brothers and it came to me that I was going too slow for the other people." She put her car keys up for good when she got home. She was "91 or 92." She's never ridden an airplane, though. "I don't want to go, thank you."

But she'll go "anywhere the bus or train goes."

(July 13, 1997)

A Happening That's
Lasted 124 Years

SCOTTSBORO -- The passionate cry of Percy Sledge singing "When a Man Loves a Woman" rolled from a Rock-Ola on the sidewalk outside Payne's. Vendors and visitors ringed the square across the street.

On a sun-splashed Sunday in Jackson County, another First Monday weekend was under way. People have gathered here for 124 years to trade dogs and lies, and if it isn't now what it was intended to be, it still goes strong. Locals called it a trade day when it started in 1868, because that's exactly what they did.

It began innocently enough. When Circuit Court went into session on the first Monday in March and then again in September, people participating in or spectating court events began to swap stuff. Horses were mainly bartered, but dogs, knives and guns quickly became favored items, too.

Over the years, the name First Monday stuck, and instead of waiting for court sessions traders congregated on the square the first Monday of every month.

They still do. Sunday there were as many car tags from Alabama counties outside Jackson as there were from inside, and a better-than-fair-share of Georgia and Tennessee license plates were seen. Vendors, or traders, ranged from first-time rookies to lifetime veterans.

But very little "trading" goes on. Unlike the old days, First Monday has become a giant flea market, yard sale, or garage sale, take your pick. Yet atmosphere and ambience remain Southern traditional.

You can still swap a dog, a gun, or a knife, but you can also buy one of those items if you don't have one to trade.

And most of today's prices are set, which means you can't often haggle with a trader to get the price lowered.

One woman Sunday picked up a $1 ceramic rabbit, asked the vendor if she'd take 50 cents for it, and was told, "No, Hon, I've got to have a dollar." If you want it, chances are you'll find it at First Monday, which has become so famous a song has been written about it. `Have you been to First Monday in Scottsboro, Alybam ..." is how the main verse goes. Not exactly Percy Sledge coming out of a Rock-Ola, but not bad when backed by mandolins and fiddles.

Mayor Walter Hammer, who has seen a large number of First Mondays, tells this story about when he worked for a wholesale drug company in

Chattanooga: "I was in one of the Northern states at a plant that did business with me, and I passed through a room where they were doing research on dogs. I asked where they got the dogs and a fellow said, `There's this little town in Alabama called Scottsboro. We go down there and get all we want.' " That was 20 years ago. Yankees don't come here to get dogs for research anymore. But Yankees, Rebels, and everybody else can get everything from parched peanuts to antiques to plain junk on the courthouse square and the streets around it.

Plus, First Monday is still a mecca for that greatest of all trade bait, gossip.

Two ladies enjoying a sunny stroll Sunday exchanged this news: "Oh, I thought she got a divorce!" exclaimed one.

"No, he passed away," explained the other.

First Monday. It just happens. Which makes it a historical happening.

(April 7, 1992)

280

About the Author

Bill Easterling has written a daily human-interest column in *The Huntsville Times* since 1978. He has won various state and national writing awards and is a member of the Alabama Sports Writers Hall of Fame.